PROFESSIONAL STRATEGIES FOR RETAIL INVESTORS

INVESTING THAT MAKES SENSE
AND
MONEY

Written by

Damir Dadachov

Copyright © 2018 by Damir Dadachov.

All Rights Reserved.

Contents

Introduction

Chapter 1: Becoming an Investor Today

Chapter 2: Getting Started

Chapter 3: Market Capitalization

Chapter 4: Timing and Opportunity

Chapter 5: Variables in Your Control

Chapter 6: The Transfer of Money

Chapter 7: Managing Risk

Chapter 8: Stock Manipulation

Chapter 9: "Blue-Chip" Stocks

Chapter 10: Taking Advantage of Over-Reactions

Chapter 11: The Power of Available Cash

Chapter 12: A Rookie Mistake

Chapter 13: Cambridge Analytica and Facebook

Chapter 14: The 2008 Financial Crisis

Chapter 15: Running a Business

Chapter 16: Money Management and Compounding

Chapter 17: A Deeper Look into An Investment

Chapter 18: Reading the Income Statement

Chapter 19: Reading the Balance Sheet

Chapter 20: The P/E Ratio and Earnings Per Share (EPS)

Chapter 21: eBay – Business Model

Chapter 22: eBay – Fundamental and Technical Analysis

Chapter 23: Building an Investment Portfolio (Part 1)

Chapter 24: Quantity, Probability, and Familiarization

Chapter 25: The Baseball Analogy

Chapter 26: Investing in an Emerging Company (HUYA)

Chapter 27: Selling Your Investments and Locking in Profits

Chapter 28: The Professional Investor

Chapter 29: Building an Investment Portfolio (Part 2)

Chapter 30: Perception Part 1 (A Shift in Confidence)

Chapter 31: Perception Part 2 (Hammer and Nail)

Chapter 32: General Investment Rules

Chapter 33: Dividend Reinvestment and Compound Interest

Final Thoughts

References List

Introduction

The reason you have purchased this book is you are interested and determined to succeed in the stock market. So, you have already taken the first smart step towards financial independence and freedom. However, making money in the stock market is far from easy and requires one to be skeptical, analytical, not be greedy, very patient, and maybe most of all an opportunist. Good investing is not gambling; it's a highly strategic art that requires patience, consistency, and strong discipline.

This book will be short and precise. A lot of books on investing are so long that a reader will get halfway through the book and simply put it down and never return to it again. My goal in this book is to present investors with clear and to the point strategies for consistent success in the stock market. I will not cover every way to money in the stock market, but I will thoroughly teach you strategies that have worked for me and have brought me consistent results. After you read this book you will come away with a clear idea and perspective on how to make money investing. Every investor has a unique approach on achieving success in the stock market; this is mine and I hope you enjoy the book and learn a lot.

Copyright © 2018 by Damir Dadachov.

All Rights Reserved.

Chapter 1: Becoming an Investor Today

The motives for someone to enter the financial markets can vary widely. You may be looking to generate some extra income on top of your job. Or you may look at the stock market as a way to ultimately generate enough wealth where you would no longer have to work a regular job. I don't like describing this as a beginner's book, but rather a book that will teach any level of investor how to be a consistent money maker. Whatever your financial goals are, the investment strategies I will present to you within this book will work for you. It does not matter the scale that you want to grow to in the stock market. A good investment strategy will work for an investor with a few thousand dollars to one with a few million dollars.

Deciding to enter the financial markets is a worthy decision in itself. Forget about performing technical analysis on stock charts, trying to predict future trends, and analyzing company financials for now; that's all part of the game but the stock market will teach you much more. The stock market happens to be one of the greatest teachers in life. The more time you spend in the markets the more you will learn about patience and reward, doing you research, not jumping to conclusions, and taking advantage of opportunities.

The market exposes a person to human behavior, how it works, and how easily it can be manipulated when money is involved. I often tell people if they want to learn very quickly about what to do and what not to do in life; they should spend six months in the stock market. The lessons you'll learn in this book and by exposing yourself to the stock market will become valuable tools in all aspects of your life.

So, how does an investor enter the stock market today in 2018? Today it is very easy to enter the stock market. Twenty-five to thirty years ago you could not sit in front of your computer while using your internet and sign up for a trading account. It was a much more elaborate process and one that was not as transparent as it is today. You would have to call a stock broker if you wanted to purchase shares of a company; and getting access to the real time stock price was not as simple as looking at your computer screen or phone app. Today, after you choose your trading platform, verify your bank account, and a few personal details with the trading platform of your choice - you are off to the races. Anyone who wants to take more control of their financial future should be in the stock market and become involved in some type of investing.

Think about the fact that in 2018 there are still billions of people around the world with no computer and no internet access. Those of us who have access to a computer and the internet are in an extremely privileged position and we should take advantage of this great opportunity. You will see the word opportunity becoming a recurring word and theme in this book. These days you can easily see the real time stock price of any company you desire just by looking at a stock app on your phone or your computer. You can just as easily look through the company's financial statements and all their reports. You can do this because we live in the information age of easily accessible data through the internet. Never before in history has the average retail investor had access to such a large pool of information as the modern retail investor does today.

Just type in the stock symbol for a company and you will get dozens of results. Results showing the current stock prices, financial statements, company news, current holders of the shares, the P/E ratio, future company endeavors, analyst predictions and so much more. I urge anyone from my friends, family, and people I meet to enter the stock market. At this point in history we have a great opportunity with current technology to make an extremely positive impact on our financial future in the markets. But, I tell everyone it's the art of timing and patience that will ultimately make them a successful and consistently profitable investor. So, I urge you to also enter the financial markets and understand that being a successful investor is very doable indeed.

Chapter 2: Getting Started

Over many decades the stock market has acquired a reputation of being a highly manipulated and corrupt place where the big institutional investors and hedge funds make billions of dollars while the average retail investor loses, and ultimately gets crushed. However, it simply does not have to be like this for you and any other average retail investor trying to take more control over their finances and build a bright future for themselves and their families in the financial markets. In this book I will teach you how to make highly calculated decisions when making an investment. The stock market is not a casino where one throws the dice and hopes for the best. Those that buy stocks based on feeling and emotion or rolling the dice, will surely lose most of the time.

There are thousands of publicly traded companies in the stock market. Some companies have multibillion-dollar market capitalizations while other companies may have market capitalizations of only a few million dollars. Some stocks trade for more than $1,000 per share while others trade for pennies on the dollar. All stocks present some amount of risk and there is no investment that is completely risk-free. Ultimately it will be up to you to make calculative and precise decisions on which stock you want to invest your hard-earned money in. You are in the stock market to win; never forget that.

After reading this book I want you to walk away with a different outlook on the stock market. Not one of negativity, impossibility, and corruption but rather one of hope and reality. It is crucial to understand that every stock has a company behind it. Whether the stock is trading for $1,000 per share or a few pennies per share; there is always a company behind a stock. Each company has sales figures, products, services, financial statements, employees, and either a bright, stagnant, or dismal future.

My objective is to teach you how to pick not only the companies with a bright future but also those that have already succeeded and are prone to present buying opportunities occasionally you can capitalize on. Investing in big established companies is one of my principal investment philosophies. These companies have proven themselves over decades in terms of profitability, resilience, and good management. It will be up to you to spot and take advantage of opportunities in their stock price. I will also teach you how to invest in up and coming companies which pose much more risk; but through certain criteria and risk management you can potentially score big on a promising company's stock.

      Once you become an investor it will also make you much more aware of money and your own financial situation. I have introduced many people over the years to the stock market and I have always seen a change come about in them. Within weeks they begin to realize the opportunity of making money by doing some research and analysis is exciting and extremely rewarding. People also begin to think about how much money they have saved and how best to manage it. I've known countless people that once introduced to the stock market became much better savers and responsible people in general. The stock market has a way of taking hold of you and forcing you to become more responsible, patient, business savvy, and a more analytical person. All these qualities can help you not just in the stock market but in most aspects of life.

Chapter 3: Market Capitalization

As a beginning exercise make a mental list of 15-20 companies you know off the top of your head; think of big and well-known companies. These companies are referred to as blue-chip companies. Blue-chip companies are large well known and established companies like Home Depot (HD), Walmart (WMT), Coca-Cola (KO), Apple (APPL) and the Kraft Heinz Company (KHC). These companies often have multibillion-dollar market capitalizations and are relatively safe investments if you know what you are doing. We will get back to these blue-chip companies in a little while.

Note: Market Capitalization = (stock price x total number of outstanding shares)

Example: If Company ABC has a current stock price of $20.65 per share, with a total of 1 million outstanding shares; the market capitalization of Company ABC is $20,650,000.

Chapter 4: Timing and Opportunity

Let's say you have a 2015 Honda Accord, grey, 100,000 miles, automatic etc. Your friend has the exact same car; same mileage, color etc. You are given the task to sell your car in two weeks for the best possible price and your friend is given two months to sell his car at the best possible price. Who do you think is more likely to get the higher price for their car? If you said the friend, you are correct. Why? The answer comes down to time and opportunity, the basis of making money in the stock market. With time comes opportunities. The stock market is all about opportunities and timing, not fast paced gambling back and forth.

The reason your friend would probably get the higher price is because he has the advantage of time on his hands. In two weeks, you must sell the car. You and your friend both advertise each car for $5,000. You want $5,000 but out of the 100 people that see your car advertisement the highest offer you get is $4,300. Your friend has more time, so he has 300 people see his ad and gets an offer of $4,900. This example can be applied directly to the stock market. With more time, opportunities present themselves at a higher rate of probability and profitability; weather to buy a stock cheaply or sell at the best possible price.

The same principal can be applied if instead of selling a car, the task was to buy a car with the same specifications in a two-week window versus a four-week window of time. Time presents patient investors with opportunity to get the best possible price on the buy and/or sell side of a transaction.

Let's begin applying the concepts of opportunity and timing to investing. Let's assume you have been looking at the Home Depot (HD) stock. You pull up a stock chart and see that approximately three months ago the price was hovering around $150 per share. Over the course of the last three months to the present time the stock price had a relatively steady climb up to $180 per share, with small fluctuations in stock price along the way. The stock would be up one day, down the next three days, up the next two etc. however the general trend for the last three months has been upwards from $150 to $180 per share.

Let's suppose that at the end of the 3-month period the stock hits an all-time high of $180 per share. As an investor what do you do? Well its being climbing steadily so you may consider it a good time to buy presuming it will continue the rising trend. That would be a possible approach, but a somewhat risky one. Avoid trying to catch a stock that's on the rise (or at its peak price), because $180 per share could be the very top for a while and you may be stuck in your position for an extended period of time. This can be incredibly frustrating and discouraging. Of course, if there is a strong argument for future growth in the company we can buy a stock near the top; this is a topic we will cover in further reading. When buying any stock in the market you must always look for the greatest possible bargain on the share price. When buying anything from a new jacket to a car, it's always wise to search for a bargain to get your money's worth; the same goes for buying stocks.

When considering buying any stock an investor must make a strong case on why the stock would be a good investment to generate profits, while presenting limited downside risk. You continue researching Home Depot (HD) stock and investigate the company's financial statements. The year over year (YOY) revenue (net sales) have being increasing or relatively stable and the company makes a good percent net profit margin every year/quarter (so they are making a certain percentage in profit on their overall sales). You look at their balance sheet and income statement and it looks relatively healthy.

However, you still should not necessarily buy at $180 per share, but now you have made a few strong points for a potential investment.

1. Home Depot (HD) is an established company that has performed well for many years and has a proven track record.

2. Strong and improving financials usually indicate that a company is doing well and is poised for growth and a promising future.

Now, we must look at the P/E ratio; is the company overvalued or not. Generally speaking, a P/E ratio of 25 and below signals that a company's stock is priced reasonably (not overpriced). We will discuss the importance of P/E (price/earnings ratio) later in the book. So, basically after a quick analysis you have determined the financial strength of the company and whether the stock is undervalued, priced well, or over valued by looking at the P/E ratio. The P/E ratio is also indicative of how much future growth investors expect a company to deliver in years to come.

In most cases, high P/E ratios indicate that investors are willing to pay more per share relative to a company's earnings per share (EPS), because they are predicting growth of the company in the future. On the other hand, a low P/E ratio may indicate that investors believe that growth in a company has stagnated or is limited, so they are not willing to pay as much per share relative to earnings per share (EPS). This is just an introduction to the concepts of the P/E ratio and earnings per share (EPS); we will discuss both terms in more detail in the coming chapters.

Let's assume you find that Home Depot (HD) is trading at a P/E ratio of 22 (at the current peak price of $180/share); which is not very cheap but is not outrageously expensive either. When I say "not very cheap" I am referring to the P/E ratio of 22. The P/E ratio is often referred to as the price multiple because it gives us a definitive value on the ratio that exists between the current share price and the earnings per share (EPS) of the company. You do some more research and find that the company's revenue has been rising for six consecutive years (2013-2018); this data can be found in the company's income statement. This information can be found through a straight forward web search and is actually the case for Home Depot (HD). Considering overall strong financials, and reasonably priced shares according to the P/E ratio you have made some good cases for potentially buying the stock.

After assessing the fundamentals of the company, we are one step closer to deciding on a possible investment. Based on strong financials and a reasonable P/E ratio an investment in HD stock may be a good decision. However, sometimes strong company fundamentals are not a strong enough case to warrant a purchase of a stock at its peak price ($180 per share in our Home Depot example). So, next comes the timing aspect of making a solid investment.

Every stock whether a stock of a solid blue-chip company like Home Depot (HD) or Walmart (WMT), or a penny stock trading for 50 cents per share presents good investment opportunities with time. For example, one day you wake up in the morning and see that Home Depot (HD) stock has fallen from a price of $180 per share to $173 per share. Curious on what might have caused the drop-in share price you begin doing some research.

You discover that Lowe's Companies Inc (LOW), another home improvement chain has issued a bad financial quarterly report and its news have rippled through the market and caused a selloff in similar stocks in its sector; Home Depot (HD) being one of those stocks. Now, this news is not directly related to Home Depot (HD); which in our case is good. Or perhaps there's something in the news about China and how their growth could impact the US economy in a negative way. There are various reasons why stocks go down in price even though the company itself has not released any bad news directly.

Events like these are common place and usually lead to investment opportunities. Why are events like those mentioned above investment opportunities? Two words – over reactions. Remember the stock market is comprised of people like you and me. Some with $1,000, some with $10,000, some with $1,000,000; and then big institutional investors and hedge funds with multi-millions or billions of dollars. Most over reactions are caused by retail investors like you and me seeing news that is perceived as "bad"; panicking and selling shares. Stocks move up and down based on the principals of supply and demand. If there are more shares being sold than shares willing to be bought by future investors in a given time frame the price will go down and vice versa. When there is a large sell-off in shares the stock is referred to as "oversold"; especially in over-reaction scenarios where the selloff is largely unwarranted.

Let's go back to our example where Home Depot (HD) stock drops to $173 per share on a sharp decline. You're now watching the stock very closely looking for just the right opportunity to execute a buy. The following should be your reasoning on why it's potentially a good buying opportunity (besides the fundamental analysis you have already performed on the company). The stock was just at $180 per share. It fell to $173 per share on an overreaction to an event that caused unjustified panic among investors and the event was not directly related to the stock. Should you now buy at $173 per share?

Well the question is; what percentage of the drop-in share price can be realistically recovered? A drop from $180 per share to $173 per share is approximately a 4% drop in price. Considering $180 per share was the recent high I would not necessarily justify a 4% drop in price as a great buying opportunity. Remember timing and patience is what will make you money in the stock market.

You could take a risk and buy at $173 per share. However, what an experienced investor will do is give it some more time. Or an experienced investor may enter with a reduced position size at $173 per share to reduce their overall risk and wait to see what plays out before buying more shares and increasing their position. Once again, if the overall trend in a stock has been upwards and all other fundamentals line up; it would be a good idea to buy in on an overreaction scenario like this one because there is probably more upside to the stock even beyond its former peak price.

There is a significant possibility the stock may drop to around $165 per share in the following days based on more panic selling and a change in overall perception of the stock. Spend enough time in the stock market and you will notice that the market tends to "over-do things" on a regular basis. Meaning good news or overall strong market sentiment may send most stocks soaring to new highs deep into overpriced territory (unreasonably high P/E ratios; or in contrast bad news or an overall "weak" or "shaky" market may send many stocks into deep decline and into bargain price territory). This happens all the time and leaves investors wishing they had waited just a little longer and not jumped the gun and bought shares. So, in this example if you just waited instead of buying at $173 per share and you bought at $165 per share, you just saved yourself approximately an additional 4.7% (the difference between $173 and $165 = 4.7%); just by waiting.

There's an acronym for investors falling prematurely to buying pressure in the stock market; FOMO or "fear of missing out". Eager investors think that if they don't buy this very instant they will miss out on a big stock run or miss a good opportunity. This mentality can be a double-edged sword and get you in some serious trouble. Sometimes it's best to sit back and do nothing and wait to see what unfolds. Maybe you did miss a great opportunity or perhaps the price will continue to drop to a level where it's almost guaranteed to make a sizeable recovery in share price over time. It's sometimes best to miss the train, another one will come sooner or later.

Over the years I have learned the great importance of good timing and patience. Genuinely good investment opportunities only come occasionally, and you must capitalize on these opportunities. Think of these events as the stocks going on sale at a local store for perhaps 10-15% off. You can do all the technical and fundamental analysis you want on a given company; however, timing and patience are the most valuable tools you have as an investor to solidify your gains and be a consistent and profitable money maker.

I have come across one quote over the years that best summarizes the art of patience in the stock market. This quote was said by famous investor Warren Buffet, the quote reads; "The stock market is a device for transferring money from the impatient to the patient,"

Warren Buffet. This quote sums up in entirety the art of patience in the stock market. Warren Buffet in countless interviews has said that good investing is boring. From retail investors to hedge fund managers; investors at all levels are prone to succumbing to boredom. To alleviate their boredom in the markets they buy in and out of stocks far too frequently looking for more excitement. Unfortunately, good investing is the art of strict discipline and patience; not a casino like experience for instant gratification and pleasure seekers.

Chapter 5: Variables in Your Control

There are countless books and so-called experts discussing how to succeed in day trading. However, statistics show that day trading only works 20% of the time. In day trading an investor does not hold onto their position beyond the current trading day. Meaning, you get into a position at some point on Monday and you're out of that position before market close at 4:00pm. What novice investors don't understand is that the volatility of a stock during a single trading day is almost impossible to predict. Day trading is just another lazy attempt to make quick profits with as little effort and patience as possible.

The lure of potentially instant profits in day trading has lost countless day traders' money and has given them a false narrative on how consistent money is made in the stock market. Trying to day trade successfully is basically trying to predict how investors that are either already invested in a stock or looking at the stock as a possible investment will behave during a six-and-a-half-hour period (from market open to close). It's almost impossible and anyone telling you different is either clueless themselves or taking you for a ride. Stay away from day trading; it's extremely risky and will most likely cause you to shut down your trading account after you suffer significant and steady losses.

I always tell people that timing and patience are probably the most important aspects of being a successful investor. Think about the complexity of the stock market and all the factors (internal and external) that could potentially influence the stock price of a company. Anything from a world event, slightly missed revenue on a quarterly report, to a news segment stating how bad the countries' unemployment figures are; could skew hundreds of stock prices in the financial markets. Your aim as an investor is to keep a cool and level head. One of the things I like to ask people to think of are the variables they can and cannot control as investors. As an investor one variable you can definitely control is your timing. The timing to either buy a stock or give it more time; or to sell a stock or give it more time.

Always keep a mental note and remember that no one can force you to buy or sell a stock; the decision to execute a trade is ultimately up to you. I have seen countless times when investors get eager and buy a stock only to see it drop 3-4% one hour after they bought it and another 5% the following day. Investors often must wait weeks or months just for the stock to recover to their original buy price and ultimately longer to reign in a profit. Sometimes it is best to sit on the sidelines and not pull the trigger on a stock. It can save you time, money, and a lot of aggravation. Patience and timing are two variables an investor has in their control in the stock market. Bottom line is, take advantage of variables you can control.

Another problem that often arises is investors grow frustrated with the stock market and try to create a set-in stone formula on how to trade different situations. You will come across books that claim to have devised a secret formula to use that will make you a winner in the stock market. Investors generally try to come up with these set-in stone formulas when they become frustrated in the unpredictability of the stock market. They don't want to think, be analytical, and patient when trying to decide whether to buy, hold, or sell a stock.

What they are looking for is to dedicate their time for a short while and ultimately come up with a formula that will make their investment life easier. Basically, a plug and play solution that will solve all their problems in the stock market. I regret to inform you; this approach never ever works and anyone or any book peddling the idea of a secret formula is a blatant lie and misinformation. The stock market is not an exact science, it's the art of exercising patience and reading into human mentality. Every stock must be assessed on an individual basis.

A key point to understand is that as a retail investor you are not in control of what happens in the stock market. Your job is to take a reactionary approach to what occurs in the stock market. There a multibillion-dollar hedge funds and institutional investors in the exact same playing field you are in. They will do anything in their power to pull the strings of the stock market to try to sway it in a favorable direction for themselves. Large institutional investors have a game plan to get in and out of a stock; only they know their game plan and the exact time they plan to execute their strategy; you're not invited to the meeting. Retail investors are the herring in an ocean full of sharks and killer whales.

I'm not degrading the retail investor but rather injecting a dose of reality that will take you down the path of success. You could be looking at a stock and suddenly see the trading volume increasing rapidly and the share price start dropping briskly on no news and for no distinct reason. Well, you're probably on the other side of a game plan being executed by a large hedge fund; where they decide to take their profits in a stock and begin unloading their multimillion-dollar position driving the stock price down (supply and demand).

Chapter 6: The Transfer of Money

Let's do some analysis on the quote; "The stock market is a device for transferring money from the impatient to the patient" Warren Buffet; and understand the meaning and value behind it. Let's go back to our Home Depot (HD) example and assume you made a commitment and bought 50 shares of Home Depot (HD) stock at $165 per share. So, you have made a total investment of $8,250.

Let's assume you bought on a Tuesday and the next trading week was a slow and rather uneventful week where the stock only moved up to a peak price of $169 per share. You became inpatient at the end of the week and sold your entire position at $167 per share. You made a profit of 1.2% (a $99 profit) on your original investment, not a bad return in a weeks' time; but not necessarily the best decision. Essentially you have sold your shares to a willing buyer at a share price which possibly has more potential to rise and provide higher percent yields in time. The stock market is an exchange of shares between buyers and sellers, some more patient and bargain conscious then others. Later in the book we will discuss an optimal strategy of getting out of your positions, locking in profits, and minimizing risk in the process.

The stock was recently trading at $180 per share, there's a fair chance it will return to that price or at least close to it. Remember the stock was trading at a P/E of 22 which makes the stock reasonably priced even at the recent peak price of $180 per share. Now, if the company was trading at a P/E of 65 you would have to reevaluate the chance of the stock rising back to its peak price and most likely have to take profits sooner. At a P/E of 65 the peak price of $180 per share is not necessarily presenting a bargain price/value for the stock because of the high P/E ratio (unless high growth is expected for the company in the near future).

Usually companies with a high P/E ratio (above 25-30) are priced for growth or have simply been overbought and mispriced by the market. Meaning investors are willing to pay more for each share as compared to the company's actual earnings per share (EPS); predicting increased and steady growth for the company in the future. Remember the P/E ratio puts a numerical value on how good of a bargain a stock is based on the price per share; we will discuss P/E ratio in further detail and how it's calculated later on.

The following week you look at your mobile device stock app and see that Home Depot (HD) stock is now at $175 per share. Of course, you should not always expect the stock to return to it's all time high, but rather set realistic expectations. That's an example of where patience would have worked to your advantage. However, you still made a profit which is an overall good scenario.

Like we mentioned earlier unrelated news can drag stocks down often creating good investment opportunities. Remember, nothing about the company you are invested in or looking at as a potential investment has changed as a result of the "unrelated news" (as far as revenues, business model etc.). Therefore, the stock price will likely make a comeback sooner or later especially if the stock is trading at a reasonable P/E ratio (among other factors like rising revenues, strong profit margins, potential for growth, and net income; like in the case of Home Depot).

Blue-chip stocks tend to rebound consistently from over-reactions due to overall high confidence among investors in the company/stock to perform over time. The ability for these types of strong and established companies to rebound from adverse reactions and return profits to investors is one of the core principles behind my investment philosophy. Investor confidence and perception in these kinds of companies tends to be high. If there is news of emerging political tensions between the USA and some other country this news may affect the financial markets as a whole. But remember, nothing about a particular company has changed after the news segment has broken. For example, bargain savvy shoppers suddenly won't stop going to Walmart (WMT) and cease buying essentials like clothes and food; reducing the company's revenue/sales.

Sometimes even after buying a stock at a bargain price the price doesn't immediately turn in the right direction. Weeks could pass before an acceptable profit is realized by an investor. In scenarios like this you often must remind yourself why you bought the stock in the first place. The purchase was warranted through a multi-step process from company financials analysis, P/E ratio analysis, and the fact that an overreaction took place. In this situation you should hold firm on your position and wait for the stock to recover at which point you may take a profit. Understand that you're not necessarily looking for the stock to recover to all-time highs, but rather a solid percentage that your satisfied with.

Chapter 7: Managing Risk

Becoming a successful investor requires one to manage their risk. Let's talk about risk management, what it means and how to best manage your investments while avoiding unnecessary risk. The stock market will present you with a lot of information and news; ultimately it will be up to you to block out certain noise and consider the big picture and what is actually important. You will see articles written about a stock, members on a stock board talking about a stock, and you may even hear your stock mentioned on CNBC; however, you have the responsibility of plucking out the important information to make a well-informed low risk investment.

Think about the car you own or maybe the house the you have recently purchased. These are possessions you have that you want to protect as much as you possibly can. Besides the legal reasons, insuring your car ultimately protects you financially in case of an accident or any event that may cause you to spend money on the car. Same with house insurance; sure, not all aspects of a house or car will be covered like new tires or a new kitchen faucet; however, a disaster or an uncontrolled event may be covered by your insurance. Insurance for your house or car is a form of risk management.

You will hear professional investors constantly using the term 'risk management' when discussing their investment portfolios and strategies. Just like you protect your bank account from significantly decreasing by insuring your car and house, you must also protect the money you put into your investments when buying and/or selling stocks. Without risk management one can quickly lose money and shut down their trading account within several months. The main difference between retail investors and professional investors is; most retail investors employ little to no risk management.

Whenever making an investment the upside reward should greatly outweigh the downside risk. One of the most important investment rules professional investors put emphasis on is capital preservation. Their number one goal is to first preserve the money that they already have. Making money comes secondary to first preserving the initial capital you have in your investment account. When buying any stock, you must first generate a thorough checklist of criteria the stock must meet before you can warrant an investment.

Let's briefly talk about a scenario that occurred where a large amount of people did not exercise risk management and have paid a big price for it. Bitcoin, the cryptocurrency - at one point had many people thinking that it would be their ticket to riches. The price of bitcoin moved upward very quickly causing gullible investors to buy bitcoin thinking that they would get rich quickly. Some people did very well but ultimately most bitcoin investors got burnt and hurt themselves financially.

Some very early investors did very well; assuming they had enough sense and sold at some point along the way. Most of that came down to luck of getting in at the beginning of the craze. However, when Bitcoin became somewhat expensive, it started to rise very rapidly (because of increasing demand) and people still bought hoping to ride out the wave on their way to riches. What they did not do is perform much or any risk management on the asset they were purchasing. Most people assumed that if bitcoin was moving steadily upwards they should also hop on the train and ride it out to the top. Unfortunately chasing a rising trend with no fundamentals behind it is probably one of the best ways to lose money. Many people bought near the top assuming that Bitcoin would keep soaring higher and higher. Unfortunately, after hitting all-time highs the value soon began to decrease rapidly.

Approaching Bitcoin from a risk management perspective would force you to ask fundamental questions about the safety of the investment. One of the first questions and concerns that should have come up when analyzing Bitcoin is whether the upwards trend in price had any real justification. Upon closer inspection it was clear to see that the rapid increase in the price of Bitcoin was simply a speculative bubble that was ready to burst. Bitcoin, unlike a company on the publicly traded stock market or even a private company has no products, no sales, no real-estate or manufacturing facility, and no actual worth. Some people argue that the real value in Bitcoin was its modern and convenient approach for purchasing things and the untraceable nature behind its transactions.

Bitcoin began as a technology or tool to facilitate quick, easy, and untraceable transactions which took away transaction fees and waiting times associated with traditional banking techniques. However, what Bitcoin quickly turned into was a speculative investment tool and an extremely risky gambling instrument rather than a modern currency and transaction tool. People thought of Bitcoin as a revolutionary and disruptive financial instrument that would be game changing and make them a lot of money. Unfortunately, for most investors the only thing that would be disrupted is their financial situation in a very negative way.

The price action of Bitcoin reflected whatever the next person or people were willing to pay for it; all speculation as opposed to investing. If you thought Bitcoin was going to continue moving higher you bought it from somebody. This snow balled into thousands or millions of people doing this with the same basic get rich quick mentality. Based on the laws of supply and demand the price of Bitcoin began to rise. The more people that wanted in on the action, the higher the demand for Bitcoin became.

Bitcoin once again is not a company; there are no sales figures and financial balance sheets an investor can analyze and decide whether to invest. I use the example of Bitcoin, which eventually dropped sharply from its peak prices and continues to be on "shaky" ground as a lesson of not implementing basic research and risk management skills. Whenever making any investment there must be fundamentals and data that can be analyzed to make a well-informed investment decision. No true justification could be made for Bitcoin rising in price besides hopeful speculation.

There are two main categories risk management can be broken down into. First, is researching the fundamentals behind whatever you are investing in and gaining an overall understanding for what is being invested in. The second part of risk management is deciding how much money (capital) to put towards an investment (limiting position size). In the case of Bitcoin, most people not only did not understand what they were investing in, but also many people had basically put their entire life savings into Bitcoin. They made the two fatal errors of investing; not researching and understanding what you are investing in and placing no emphasis on the position size of the investment. Many people put a large percentage of their savings into Bitcoin, an amount of money they simply could not afford to lose.

I remember as Bitcoin was rapidly rising, quite a few people asked me what I thought about it and if they should buy it. I told them to stay as far away from Bitcoin and other cryptocurrencies as possible because the price action of these cryptocurrencies is almost impossible to predict. I explained to people that trying to evaluate Bitcoin and where it would go next is almost impossible and a foolish endeavor, because there was nothing to evaluate as far as core fundamentals and data. I personally refuse to invest into something that I cannot analyze based on data and fundamentals.

Chapter 8: Stock Manipulation

Now, let's talk about a subject that is essential to understanding the stock market. Stock manipulation is a harsh reality in the stock market. Manipulation should not be overlooked when forming an opinion on a stock and should be part of your research process when making an investment decision. Manipulation of the stock prices is illegal and has serious consequences; in accordance to the Securities and Exchange Commission (SEC). However, some forms of stock manipulation are subtler then others and may be harder to read for the novice investor. "Market manipulation is a deliberate attempt to interfere with the free and fair operation of the market and create artificial, false or misleading appearances with respect to the price of, or market for, a stock, commodity or currency." "Market manipulation." *Wikipedia*. Wikimedia Foundation Inc, 22 May 2018. Web. 15 Sept 2018. https://en.wikipedia.org/wiki/Market_manipulation

As investors in the modern age we are exposed to a constant flow of news, opinions, and discussion on stocks. A lot of opinions and discussions about stocks happen on online stock boards. We must take in all this information with a filter and not be influenced by every view presented about a stock. Let's assume a hedge fund has a position in stock ABC; the fund is long on the position meaning they want the stock to rise as high as possible for maximum profit. They may put up a post masquerading as an individual investor on a stock board complementing the stock and saying how bright its future is. Meanwhile, they may not actually believe this but are hoping for enough people to be influenced by the post and buy the stock. When there are a lot of willing buyers and the demand for shares is high (supply and demand), the stock may and probably will go upward. This plays into the hands of the person/people who wrote the manipulative post in the first place.

These posts may also work vice versa; meaning they are there to manipulate the stock in a downward direction. The post may say a company has a lot of competition and is grossly overvalued and there will be a sharp decline soon in share price. If a person or hedge fund is short on a position, they want the price of the stock to drop to make money. So, any post that helps achieve a price drop in the stock will help their cause.

Another commonly used trick on these stock boards are users posting screen shots of their trading accounts. Sometimes you will see screen shots of an actual trading account that is up 200% and shows a list of many profitable trades. The purpose of posting screen shots is for the person or organization posting the information to gain credibility and trust among investors reading the stock boards.

However, some people/organizations generating these screen shots have two separate trading accounts; one account for long positions (making money when a stock goes up in price) and the other account for short positions (making money when a stock falls in price). When the "person" makes money on the upside they post a screen shot and vice versa. They are long and short on the same stock in two different accounts. They will screen shot and post whichever position produces a positive result; convincing gullible on lookers to believe in their predictions and investments strategies.

This makes them look knowledgeable, credible, and trustworthy in their predictions. Meanwhile they have learned to play both sides of the coin; while not actually being able to predict the direction of a stock. If enough people gain confidence in the "person" generating these posts, there's a higher probability a large group of investors will follow their advice on a stock in the future. Being able to steer a significant number of investors to either buy, sell, or hold a stock can be very profitable to those making the manipulative posts.

What makes it even worse is that an organization may create many different user accounts on a stock board (masquerading as individual and "unrelated" investors). Several accounts telling investors to go long on a stock while other accounts telling investors to sell a stock. A percentage of investors will fall for the upside narrative while the others will fall for the narrative of the stock falling in price. This enables whoever posted the comments or screens shots to make money on both groups of investors and in either direction of the stock.

Another common type of post will say something along the lines of; "it's risky to hold the stock overnight or the weekend." To a novice investor this may seem like a reasonable thought. However, if you have done your research on a company with a strong emphasis on fundamental analysis there is nothing that makes a good investment riskier by holding it into the next trading day or over a weekend (this is not to be confused with holding a stock through quarterly earnings where there is a high chance of investors reacting to either positive or negative earnings causing the stock to move up or down in price).

"Don't hold a position over night or the weekend" are usually false narratives being posted for the sole purpose of manipulation; again, trying to influence the behavior of investors to sell a stock. Some of these posts are coming from the interest to influence investors to sell their positions in large quantities driving the stock price lower and creating an opportunity for those behind the post to enter the stock at a cheaper price. The other side of where posts like this can come from is the brokerage industry, which is incentivized by trading volume and frequency. So, the more investors buy in and out of stocks the more fees brokerages collect.

Not all these kinds of posts come from stock chat rooms/boards. Sometimes you will come across an article on the internet about a stock. Perhaps a large investment group or investment bank will issue a "buy", "sell", or "hold" rating on a stock followed by an article stating the reasons they believe this to be the case. It is important to read through these types of articles because often times they provide genuine and in-depth information about a company that otherwise would be almost impossible to find through your own research. It is important to understand that large investment groups usually have many people dedicated to researching deep into a company and finding every detail about it. As retail investors we may not have access to some of the information these large investors have access to. However, when reading anything about a stock you should always be speculative about the motive behind an article or post. Understand that a "buy" or "sell" rating maybe be issued for the sole purpose of moving the stock in the direction that benefits those behind the article or post.

With that said, stock boards and chat rooms can be very useful tools to an investor; especially an individual investor who works alone and does all their own research on stocks. As an individual investor you should constantly be looking for a good bargain on a stock that is not necessarily priced cheaply but has a promising future; like increasing sales or possible big contracts on the way. We are presented with a lot of information and possibilities in the financial markets; thousands of stocks and possible opportunities.

Some of the posts on the stock boards are genuine in nature and they may provide ideas to an investor. Maybe your research on a stock has missed an important article or piece of news that someone may post on the stock board alerting you and other investors. After reading an article or financial report you may change your opinion on a stock that will actually benefit you. As individual investors we do our own research and there is a good chance we can miss a piece of information that would be critical to us making a well-informed decision on a stock.

If you are careful and analytical you can generate ideas and find new pieces of information from these stock boards/articles. Also, sometimes a post will alert you to another stock which you otherwise may not have found. The stock may present a great opportunity and be worthwhile researching. So, the bottom line is stock boards, chatrooms, and articles possess negative and positive attributes; use them cautiously and understand that not all posts/articles have your best interest in mind.

Chapter 9: "Blue-Chip" Stocks

Earlier I mentioned blue-chip companies; let's now discuss these types of companies and the benefits associated with trading their stocks. A blue-chip is a nationally recognized, well-established, and financially sound company. "These companies largely sell high-quality, widely accepted products and services. Blue-chip companies are known to weather downturns and operate profitably in the face of adverse economic conditions, which helps to contribute to their long record of stable and reliable growth. The name "blue chip" comes from the game of poker in which the blue chips have the highest value." "Blue Chip." *Investopedia*. Investopedia, LLC., Web. 18 Sept 2018. https://www.investopedia.com/terms/b/bluechip.asp

A substantial portion of these companies can come to mind even to a non-investor. Some examples of these companies include but are not limited to; Kellogg Company (K), The Coca Cola Company (KO), General Mills, Inc (GIS), International Business Machines Corporation (IBM), The Kraft Heinz Company (KHC), United Parcel Service, Inc. (UPS), McDonald's Corporation (MCD), Walmart Inc. (WMT), Home Depot, Inc. (HD), Apple Inc. (AAPL), American Express Company (AXP), and 3M Company (MMM). This is a list of some blue-chip companies. You are probably already familiar with most of these companies, even though you may have no stock market experience.

Investing in blue-chip companies presents investors with a greater margin of safety; which inherently is good risk management. A good portion of investors in blue-chip stocks are in these investments for the long run and understand about general market corrections and possible down trends in the individual stock prices. These companies tend to be less volatile then non-established companies for this reason. A large percentage of investors in blue-chip stocks are looking for long term growth and dividend payments from the companies every quarter; decreasing their chance of selling the stock based on pure emotion and speculation (this creates less volatility).

We look for a margin of safety and perform risk management whenever buying a stock. Blue-chip companies provide a greater stability in share price and present less risk then smaller and less established companies. Their history of profitability, strong management, resilience, and durability make these companies great investments. A good portion of these companies can be found on the DJIA (Dow Jones industrial Average).

Now, let's get back to why these types of companies should be on your radar when searching for investments. One reason is these companies have proven themselves over many decades to be well run and profitable businesses that won't crash overnight. Again, this is one positive characteristic we are looking for when we do our risk assessment on a stock. Not to say that any of these companies have not seen down periods in stock price or have not experienced turbulent times. However, they generally present far less risk than a penny stock or a relatively new company that has not proven itself on a consistent basis.

One of the most positive characteristics of blue-chip companies is that they usually have a strong competitive advantage in their respective sectors making them very difficult to infiltrate. For example, a company like Walmart (WMT) has a huge number of locations. "As of January 31, 2018, Walmart has 11,718 stores and clubs in 28 countries, operating under 59 different names." "Walmart." *Wikipedia*. Wikimedia Foundation Inc, 29 Oct 2018. Web. 02 Sept 2018. https://en.wikipedia.org/wiki/Walmart

Also, consumers like to stick with brands and companies they know and trust, that present good value on their products and services. The large foot print combined with low prices on products is very difficult for competitors to infiltrate (in the case of Walmart). This makes these types of companies durable and in general safer investments then companies that don't have a strong edge over their competitors. A good portion of blue-chip companies offer products and services that are household names. Consumers have used these products/services for generations. Consumer familiarity and dependence on these large companies and their product/services gives these companies a strong competitive advantage.

These blue-chip companies usually hold the number one, two, or three positions in their sector or field of operation. Companies like these usually have strong management that focuses not only on company profitability but the wellbeing and satisfaction of their shareholders (you and me). This is another positive attribute for investing in these types of companies. That last thing these companies want is public scrutiny and dissatisfied shareholders that could affect their public image in negative way, potentially sabotaging sales and profitability.

These stocks often have reasonable P/E ratios which is an indication that their stocks are priced at a rational valuation. The P/E ratios vary on blue-chip stocks but are generally not in overpriced territory. Again, this plays into our risk assessment strategy. Generally, when we look for stocks we are looking for a bargain to lower our risk of the price dropping much further. We look for a stable company that usually is not too volatile in its stock price. And third, we look for opportunities that we can take advantage of. A good portion of these blue-chip stocks are constantly in the "spotlight" and are some of the most traded and evaluated stocks on the stock market. This usually leads to these companies being priced "efficiently." Meaning, that they have been valued at reasonable P/E ratios.

Being constantly in the "spot-light" of the stock market brings these companies large amounts of coverage and attention; from articles being written on them to constant valuations and predictions of their future. In contrast, companies that are not constantly in the "spotlight" often can get mispriced (as far as P/E ratios) by the market. Mispricing can either lead to great investment opportunities (if the market gives a company an undeserving low valuation) or can create higher risk if the company gets mispriced by the market at an unreasonably high valuation. You may say to yourself; if these blue-chip companies are already efficiently priced they probably won't present good investment opportunities because their stocks have already been priced correctly by the market.

However, it is important to understand that their efficient pricing often leads to great investment opportunities in overreaction situations where their shares fall in price. These are companies that are usually highly profitable and priced efficiently, so if an overreaction takes place and brings the stock lower, often times the stock begins to enter "bargain territory." This in turn leads to great investment opportunities because these types of stocks usually rebound back to their former share price.

Interestingly enough there is a sector in blue-chip stocks that has historically had higher volatility then other blue-chip sectors. A lot of big technology companies provide somewhat riskier but good opportunities to investors because of their more volatile nature. Though relatively safe, the blue-chip technology sector is probably the most "action packed". A large percentage of people that tend to invest in technology companies are always looking for the latest news or hottest product releases. The technology sector moves quickly due to speedy innovation and constant new product releases.

The investors that are usually attracted to technology stocks tend to sell a stock just as quickly as they buy into it, often applying little fundamental analysis behind their investments. In turn the stock price in these companies tends to be more volatile than blue-chips stocks in other sectors. This type of investing causes volatility and often leads to good investment opportunities. Volatility in the blue-chip technology sector is not to be confused with the high-risk volatility that occurs in penny stocks and unproven companies which is largely based around fear and sometimes manipulation. Of course, as an investor that performs risk management you should invest in a diverse group of companies in different sectors, not just technology - this manages our risk. These blue-chip technology stocks are still established and well managed companies. By no means are these blue-chip technology high risk stocks. I recommend that three to five technology stocks should always be on your watchlist.

A general rule that may be applied to investing in more volatile companies is as follows: invest in stocks where there are investors with similar interests (to make money) but different strategies and investment mentalities. Technology stocks and up and coming companies can often attract a significant amount of "crazy investors". A rational investor wants to compete with irrational people. Irrational investors tend to over react in upside or downside situations which often leads to opportunity for the rational and thoughtful investor. As investors our goal is always to manage risk, look for irrational and over reactive behavior, and always look to get a bargain price on a stock.

Chapter 10: Taking Advantage of Over-Reactions

To be an effective investor you must look at a substantial amount of different stocks. As I mentioned in the beginning, make a list of 15-20 blue-chips stocks that you could hypothetically follow. Now, here is where we can really talk about opportunities. Opportunities in blue-chip stocks only present themselves occasionally. Most opportunities in blue-chip stocks arise when there is a significant dip in stock price due to an overreaction. However, there is also significant possibilities to make good investments in blue-chip stocks that are exhibiting increasing revenues and are positioned to deliver strong long-term growth. In further chapters we will discuss long-term growth strategies when investing in emerging companies and blue-chip stocks that a positioned for future growth. In this chapter we will cover investing in blue-chip stocks in overreaction scenarios. In blue-chip companies your goal should be to look for significant dips in stock price caused by overreactions and/or prolonged downtrends (which eventually level off) in stock price which ultimately lead to a bargain price.

The reason opportunities like these should be taken advantage of especially in blue-chip companies lies in their ability to whether market downturns and corrections and rebound from them. Let's take Walmart (WMT) as an example and talk about its stock. Walmart is a blue-chip company with great sales and overall financials. Walmart is the largest retail chain in the U.S and has basically trumped all its competition as far as the sale of affordable clothing, food, household supplies, and electronics etc.

On Wednesday, May 9th, 2018 investors of Walmart (WMT) learned that the company had confirmed a $16 billion deal to buy a majority stake in an Indian company called Flipkart. Walmart announced it would acquire a 77% stake in Flipkart. Russell, Jon. "Walmart completes its $16 billion acquisition of Flipkart." *TechCrunch*. Oath Tech Network, August 2018. Web. 19 Sept 2018. https://techcrunch.com/2018/08/20/walmart-flipkart-deal-done/

Flipkart is an Indian e-commerce company, similar to Amazon (AMZN) but for the Indian market. Since Walmart spent such a large amount of money on this deal, the company announced that the deal could reduce Walmart's earnings by 60 cents per share (EPS- Earnings Per Share) in the next fiscal year. The major reason behind this deal was to put Walmart (WMT) into a better position to compete with Amazon (AMZN).

After this deal was announced I decided to look deeper into Walmart's (WMT) financial statements. I found that revenues from 2009 through 2017 had steadily increased year over year. By pulling up a stock chart I can see that Walmart's (WMT) share price was around $109 per share (an all-time high in the company's stock price) as of January 29, 2018. The price had slid down over the following five months since late January 2018 to the mid-low $80's per share. Nothing bad had happened with the company but rather most stocks in the market fell organically as a large percentage of established companies' stocks seemed to peak around the end of January 2018 (this is referred to as a market correction). Now, I want to look at the current P/E ratio to see if the stock is presenting a good value at the current share price. I see the current P/E is 17.48. This is a very reasonable P/E ratio; usually a P/E ratio of 25 and below indicates a well valued stock based on an earnings per share basis.

Let's talk about what happened immediately after the Flipkart deal was announced. Shortly after the Flipkart deal was announced (May 9th, 2018), Walmart's (WMT) share price fell approximately 4% to around $82.20 per share. This drop-in share price occurred on the same day the deal was announced; I saw an immediate opportunity to buy the stock. The stock had already declined approximately 26% since its high in January 2018 (amidst consistently rising revenues and a reasonable P/E ratio).

The decline in share price was organic (not a steep fall) from an all-time high share price for the stock. Prolonged down trends or declines usually happen organically due to profit taking and an overall changed perception of the stock by the market. However, a prolonged down trend due to decreasing revenues over recent financial quarters or years is a completely different scenario (this could signal that a company is in trouble); in contrast Walmart (WMT) has had increasing revenues. This drop-in share price occurred in Walmart for two main reasons; lowered projected earnings per share (for the next year as a result of the money spent on the Flipkart deal) and a perceived notion by some investors that Walmart entered this deal in desperation to compete with e-commerce giant Amazon (AMZN).

After the share price decline the day the deal was announced I saw an opportunity and an irrational overreaction by investors. In fact, on May 9th, 2018 after the deal was announced the stock hit an intraday low of $82 per share. On June 26, 2018 the stock hit a high of $87.05 per share. From the low of $82 per share to roughly $87 per share is approximately a 6.1% gain. This is what I roughly predicted would happen; not to the exact percentage but I have seen many over reactions where investors sell and drive the stock price down to where it becomes a bargain and enters oversold territory.

Several factors made this situation a good investment opportunity. Rising company revenues, a reasonable P/E ratio, and an overreaction by investors all came together to present a strong investment opportunity in Walmart (WMT). Also, even though some investors overreacted, general investor confidence in a large and established company like Walmart is high. This is another reason I was certain that the stock would rebound after the initial drop in price. The stock closed at a price of $95.86 per share on August 31, 2018. From a low of $82 per share to approximately $96 per share is a 17% gain in an approximately 4-month period; a very good return.

This is one of many investment opportunities I have seen in blue-chip companies over the years and it would be impossible to write about them all. When I talk to people about investment strategies one of the major points I try to stress to investors is the importance of investing in blue-chip stocks when opportunities arise. Those stocks have a great ability to recover from declines in their share price. With today's mobile devices you can be viewing a huge amount of stocks on your phone with a basic stock app. I recommend that 15-20 of those stocks should be blue-chip stocks.

Irrational overreactions by investors take place all the time. Think about the large number of well-established and profitable blue-chips stocks in the stock market. In a single year at least 5 significant over reactions will take place in different blue-chip stocks varying in sectors of operation. Sometimes 2-3 overreactions will take place in a single stock during the course of a single year, presenting great investment opportunity.

Note: Sometimes it's helpful to look at a company's stock not as a buyer but as a salesman. This change of perspective can force an investor to ask themselves questions they may not have thought of regarding a stock. If you were trying to sell a potential investor on buying a stock what points and arguments would you present on why the stock is presenting a good investment opportunity. Does the company have a bright future, is the stock reasonably priced, are revenues and profit margins strong, how will consumer trends affect the revenue of the company etc.? If you cannot make a strong argument on why someone else should be an investor in a company, you should probably not be an investor either.

Chapter 11: The Power of Available Cash

Blue-chip stocks are relatively stable companies, so they do not present opportunities very frequently on an individual basis. However, by having 15-20 thoroughly selected blue-chip stocks on your phone or computer it gives an investor a higher chance of seeing an opportunity when it arises. Whether the opportunity comes from manipulation, a global event, news that's perceived as bad, increasing company earnings, or an organic drop in the share price. If an investor looked at only three blue-chip stocks, opportunities would be far and between. However, if an investor is looking at 15-20 stocks, opportunities will arise at a higher rate and probability. Once you capitalize on one or two investment opportunities, which may take a week or months to show profitability; another one or two opportunities will present themselves in other companies that are part of your watchlist (this cycle can repeat itself leading to consistent returns).

Now, let's talk a little more about putting yourself in a position to take advantage of an opportunity when it presents itself. Everyone at one point in their life comes across an opportunity that they wish they could have taken advantage of. However, often times when a prospect presents itself we are not in a position to take advantage of it.

Let's say you get a phone call from a relative one day and he tells you that he has a car that he has to get rid of. His wife just bought a new car and there's simply no space in the driveway. He offers you a great price and you drive over to his house to look at the car. You decide to bring a friend along who is a mechanic and could spot things about the car that you possibly could not (again an example of risk management). After closer inspection you and your friend conclude that the car is in great mechanical condition and has many years of life left in it. Your relative tells you the price he wants for the car and you quickly begin to realize how good of a deal it is. He needs to get rid of the car, you are related to him, and the relative is not desperate for cash; all these factors come together to give you a great deal or opportunity. You tell the relative you will think about it and get back to him.

You go home and begin to think about the car you saw and the good qualities your mechanic noticed about it. You realize that not only could the car serve as reliable and cheap transportation for years to come but you could also potentially sell the car at a higher price and earn a nice profit for yourself. You begin to realize you don't have much cash and you probably won't be able to purchase the car. Unfortunately, you are not in the position to take advantage of the opportunity and lose out on potentially flipping the car for a quick profit.

This is precisely what you do not want to happen to you as an investor in the stock market. You always should have enough cash available in your investment account to take advantage of a great opportunity. All your cash should not be tied up in different investments. A certain percentage of your account should always consist of cash. We will talk about this concept in detail in the next chapter when we discuss how to build a strong investment portfolio and the two main reasons behind having available cash in your investment account.

Chapter 12: A Rookie Mistake

The majority of novice investors open an investment account and put a few thousand dollars of their hard-earned savings into the investment account. Next, they buy two or three stocks that take up the entire amount of money that they have deposited into their account (leaving no available cash in the account). When an opportunity arises, they will dump one of their existing positions and attempt to hop on the "new" opportunity because they need capital to get into the new position. The novice investor will often sell a position they were already holding for a loss and jump into the next stock. This behavior repeats itself and often leads to consistent losses for the investor. They are not patient enough to let their prior positions mature and turn profitable. My strong advice to investors at all levels is to keep a certain percentage of your account as cash.

The two main reasons you want to keep a percentage of your account as cash are:

1. Being able to take advantage of opportunities.

2. Avoiding risk by limiting your exposure to the stock market.

In the stock market nothing is guaranteed, so by keeping a percentage of your account as cash an investor can avoid possibly throwing all their money into potentially losing investments. Also, the financial markets sometimes experience large price corrections and even outright disasters like the 2008 financial crisis. Think about the fact that on average a recession in the stock market occurs every five years. Since 1854 the U.S.A has experienced 33 recessions. Cash in your account can not be affected by these events and gives an investor a greater margin of safety (risk management).

Definitions:

Recession = When a nation has a wide economic decline that lasts for 6 months or more.

Depression = When a nation has a wide economic decline that lasts for 3 to 5 years or more.

The principal goal for any investor should be capital preservation. Many investors enter the stock market with a great sense of urgency to make money. They often make quick and irrational decisions involving far too much risk. The mentality of a good investor is first and foremost not to lose money (capital preservation), followed by making consistent and realistic profits.

Let's talk about an example of when having cash in your account can be advantageous. An investor opens an investment account and puts in a total of $6,000. The investor has spent several weeks researching various blue-chip companies and looking for investment opportunities. A few companies meet the investors criteria and the investor puts $2,000 in each company (leaving the remaining $2,000 as cash in the account). However, sometimes investments take longer than expected to produce a profit in the stock market, so the price of the two stocks does not move as quickly as the investor initially expected. The investor is now beginning to get frustrated by the time it is taking the investments to rise in price and return a profit.

One morning while surfing the web the investor sees news of a hack into Facebook's (FB) user profiles possibly compromising user information and security. He finds this interesting and checks up on Facebook's (FB) stock price which has dropped 10% on a sharp downward spike. Knowing this could signal a possible opportunity he buys $1,000 worth of Facebook (FB) shares hoping for a stock price reversal. The investor was smart for leaving a percentage of his trading account as cash; because he was able to quickly see an opportunity and an overreaction and capitalize on it. The stock rebounds quickly in price the following day and the investor walks away with a healthy 8% profit. Now, he is less frustrated with his other two positions and is less likely to make an irrational move based on boredom and frustration with the slow performing investments.

Most professional investors keep a significant percentage of their portfolios as cash. They understand that opportunities don't come often but when they arise you don't want to be the one standing on the sidelines wishing you had some free cash to make an investment. The second reason professional investors keep a significant percentage of their accounts as cash is to protect themselves in case of market crashes and large price corrections. The world of professional investing is heavily based on risk management and large margins of safety. Your investment objective is to follow the professional investor model of high margin of safety investments, limited market exposure, and limited position sizes per investment.

Chapter 13: Cambridge Analytica and Facebook

We have talked about this earlier, but it is incredibly important to stress the point of taking advantage of opportunities when they arise. When the Cambridge Analytica scandal surfaced, Facebook (FB) suffered the largest one day drop in its share price in its history. The price drop decreased the market capitalization of the company by billions of dollars. Facebook (FB) shares fell about 24% in price and the company lost roughly around $134 billion in value off its market capitalization. About two months later the stock price had recovered to where it was before the scandal. This is the reality of the stock market especially when dealing with big established companies that are giants of their industry. Investors are prone to overreact to "bad" news. Irrational reactions like these are the best opportunities for a rational investor to make money.

Large established companies generally have a solid reputation among investors. Investors trust in the ability of these companies to perform and whether downturns and difficult times. Because of this, when an overreaction takes place, often times a large percentage of the price drop caused by the overreaction can be recovered. When enough investors have this mentality (a belief that the stock will recover) the stock price will usually go up as investors begin to buy back into the stock. This phenomenon is not as consistent or pronounced in less established companies or penny stocks where the overall perception and confidence in the company is low.

The key aspect to understand about the Cambridge Analytica scandal was that it was not directly correlated to Facebook's revenue, profit margins, or even its long-term future. Yes, the scandal was not good publicity for sure, but does it really warrant a 24% decline in share price and a $134 billion market capitalization decline? The answer to this question is absolutely not. Why? Ask yourself - would you delete your Facebook account after such a scandal; and what percentage of people that you know, would or did delete their Facebook accounts? It is also key to understand that Facebook (FB) stock was trading at a very reasonable P/E ratio before the scandal took place. The stock was not in overpriced territory based on the P/E ratio. So, the huge drop in share price made the chance of share price recovery even more likely.

If I ask myself that same question the answer would be that I knew no one that deleted their account. Sure, there were users that deleted their accounts but again for a company to lose almost a quarter of its market capitalization value is a huge overreaction by shareholders. Therefore, you should take advantage of such an opportunity. Nothing is guaranteed in the stock market; the only guarantee is that opportunities will arise in stocks occasionally.

There is a saying in the stock market; "Buy the fear, sell the greed." Fear and greed are usually emotions that lead to irrational decisions and extreme actions. As a rational investor you want to compete with irrational investors. We have talked about over reactions to news and other variables and how these events can present opportunities. We have mostly covered "buying the fear" situations; however, "selling the greed" is just as important. Just like fear, greed is also largely irrational.

When investors see a stock that is moving rapidly upwards due to a good quarterly report or a newly secured contract, they tend to jump on the band wagon quickly. However, the upward momentum can end very quickly due to investors selling shares and profit taking. This can leave investors that bought on the upwards swing in a bad position as the price begins to decline briskly after the initial "pop" in share price. The rule is to sell in the beginning stages of the greed. Selling for a reasonable profit is good risk management; as opposed to waiting to realize the maximum and often unrealistic potential profits.

Chapter 14: The 2008 Financial Crisis

Let's talk about an even bigger opportunity that took place in 2008; the 2008 financial crisis. Very few people could have predicted the financial crisis of 2008 and just as few people knew how to take advantage of the opportunity it presented. However, some investors did take advantage of the opportunity and made a lot of money in the process. I strongly recommend you watch the movie The Big Short as it delves into this event. This movie shows how the research and patience of a few bright people paid off during a time of economic despair and collapse.

By no means am I saying that the financial crisis of 2008 in which thousands of jobs were lost and retirement accounts were wiped out was a good event. But there is an expression in the stock market that says; when there's blood in the streets you buy. Well there was definitely "blood" in the streets during the financial crisis. If you pull up any stock chart around 2008 what you will see is that a significant portion of all stocks hit multiple decade lows in their stock prices. This is where having a percentage of cash in your account like we mentioned earlier would have been extremely useful and advantageous. Not only could you have taken advantage of record low share prices but also decreased your exposure to falling stocks during the meltdown by having a percentage of cash not invested in anything.

The massive decline in stock prices presented a huge opportunity to buy stocks at enormous discounts. If you look at some companies whose stocks took a massive blow during the crisis you will see that months and years following the decline they all recovered in price. Some stocks even reached all-time highs years after the collapse. Opportunities like this come about very seldomly but they should be taken advantage of. However, you don't need to wait decades for a financial collapse to make money as an investor.

As we mentioned earlier stocks present opportunities on a smaller scale all the time and you should take advantage of them as much as you can. I don't want people to think that succeeding in the stock market is based upon taking advantage of other people's misfortune and suffering. But just think, at the end of the year a car dealership tries to get rid of last year's models by putting a discount on them, the stock market also presents its own discounts and opportunities periodically. When you go to the grocery store with a few coupons you are taking advantage of an opportunity. The reality is, in all business endeavors one must be financially shrewd and calculating to achieve success.

Chapter 15: Running a Business

Think of a small business like a mom and pop restaurant and how it operates. The revenue taken in by the restaurant will be divided up and spent on different necessities so that the business can stay operational. The revenue will be dedicated to many things like; payroll for employees, cooking equipment, plates/utensils, cost of food, utilities, rent, taxes and probably most important of all an "emergency fund" in case something goes wrong. For example, if a gas stove in the restaurant breaks down the entire restaurant could come to a standstill. Business owners that are smart always prepare for the future and retain a certain amount of money/capital for unexpected expenses and emergencies.

You as an investor, even on the scale of a small retail investor are essentially running a business. After all, as an investor you are obligated to pay capital gains tax at the end of the year on your realized profits. Just like the mom and pop restaurant owner, you need to have a percentage of your investment account as cash in case of an emergency or in our case a significant market correction or outright crash. You must get into the mind state of managing your investment portfolio like you would a profitable and well managed business. A business that takes calculated risks but puts an emphasis on long term survival and ultimately growth.

Having a percentage of an investment account as cash will keep an investor "liquid" and operational in the face of adverse market conditions. In case of a market crash, your core business (your investment portfolio) will be partially protected by keeping a portion of your money out of the market. When a stock market "emergency" strikes you will be able to buy new "equipment" or stocks at discount prices to keep your business afloat and moving forward; even when emergencies strike. Think of a stock market crash or correction as the "equipment" in the restaurant that breaks down.

If the owner of the restaurant has no cash reserves, the business will come to a halt and cease producing cash flow. The owner with no cash reserves cannot buy the needed equipment to replace the broken equipment to keep the restaurant bringing in cash. When the stock market crashes, most of your portfolio can essentially become "broken" for a period of time until the market recovers. If you have a cash reserve, you can buy new equipment/stocks to keep the business cash flow positive and profitable. A successful investor or business owner will always manage to stay afloat and push forward even when disaster strikes.

Chapter 16: Money Management and Compounding

Let's have a change of pace and talk about how to best manage your investment portfolio and see just how lucrative a financial instrument the stock market can be. For this example, we will assume that John (an investor), has $30,000 in his investment account. There are investors with less than that amount and there a some with a lot more; we will use this amount just as an example.

Because it's smart to perform risk management through diversification and limited position size, John splits the $30,000 into five different carefully selected investments; however, he leaves a percentage of his investment account as cash. So that would mean John has five investments, $5,000 each in value (at the beginning of each investment). John has $25,000 invested while keeping $5,000 in cash. We divide up our investments for risk management just in case a few investments take a while to produce profits or underperform; we can count on our other positions for a profit until the remaining investments recover.

Note: Before we move further let's take a look at how John has divided up his investment portfolio. Each investment is 16.6% of the total account value ($5,000 / $30,000 = 16.6%). He also has 16.6% of the total account value as cash ($5,000 / $30,000 = 16.6%).

On January 1st, 2018 John invests $5,000 in each of his five stocks. Let's assume each investment produces a 10% annual return. This does not mean John must hold each position for a year, but rather he uses $5,000 blocks to trade in and out of stocks as opportunities arise securing profits along the way. We will not assume compounding of the money in the first part of this example. Compounding would mean if John made a 5% profit on a $5,000 investment, he would now have $5,250 to reinvest again.

Assuming each of John's $5,000 investments can produce a 10% annual return; after one year each $5,000 investment would be $5,500. So, after one year of investing the $25,000 originally invested by John would be - ($5,500 x 5) $27,500. That would mean that John made a total profit of $2,500 in that year ($27,500 - $25,000 = $2,500 profit). This would bring John's total account value to $32,500 (remember the John kept $5,000 in cash).

Now let's apply the principle of compounding to our example. The next year John would have $5500 for each investment (assuming he invested in five stocks again), which at a 10% annual return would turn into $6,050 per investment. This would bring John's total account value to $35,250; ($6,050 x 5) + $5,000 cash = $35,250.

Of course, John should not put all his realized profits from the previous year into his upcoming investments, but rather take out a percentage of the profits and put them towards the cash portion of his investment account (risk management). We will cover this in further detail in later reading. If you can keep your yearly returns consistent your money will grow quickly, and profits will be larger for the same percentage realized; that's the power of the "compounding machine". The more money you have, the more money you can make with equal or even less effort. The rich get richer for good reason.

Chapter 17: A Deeper Look into An Investment

Now, let's concretely talk about an investment strategy. My principal strategy focuses on investing in blue-chip companies when opportunities arise. "Blue-chips" are usually companies with multibillion-dollar market capitalizations that have stood the test of time through a strong competitive advantage and stout management. These companies have proven themselves through their products, services, and business savvy practices over many decades.

Remember, when choosing any stock to invest in you want to make a checklist of criteria the stock must meet before you pull the trigger and justify an investment. Most blue-chip companies will provide you with the first check mark because these companies have proven themselves repeatedly over time. Investing in these companies inherently brings about good risk management due to the general stability associated with substantial and reputable companies. These are not penny stocks that have not proven themselves. The companies behind most penny stocks have lack luster management and poor financial balance sheets. The majority of penny stocks are penny stocks for good reason.

So, how should you pick a blue-chip company? The first thing you should do is make a list of some big companies that you are interested in and understand from a business perspective; companies like McDonald's (MCD), Apple (AAPL), Walmart (WMT) or Home Depot (HD). My general rule is once you have picked some blue-chip companies you should start performing fundamental analysis and researching them thoroughly (revenues, profit margin, net income, P/E ratio, assets, liabilities, cash on hand). Become familiar on how to read a balance sheet and income statement. These basic accounting principles will allow you to analyze a company much more thoroughly and understand it from the inside out.

I have always warned investors to avoid blue-chip companies that are subject to trends (when considering investing for long term growth) unless their shares are selling at a great bargain or an overreaction has taken place. An example of this would be Nike (NKE). If you look at a 10-year chart of Nike (NKE) it's basically an upwards trend; and you may say that's great and it would be a good investment. I have had Nike (NKE) stock on my radar for years; however, I have never invested in it. The main reason I have never invested in Nike (NKE) stock is because the company's business model is prone to trends. Besides doing fundamental analysis on a company I always think of three words when considering a company and the services/ products it offers. These words are: wants, needs, and trends of consumers respective to a specific company's services and products.

Think about Nike (NKE) and about the products the company sells. They sell shoes, clothing, and various other sporting equipment. I know very few people that will only buy the Nike (NKE) brand when considering there wants and/or needs as far as shoes, clothing, and other sporting gear and apparel. Sure, there are hardcore enthusiasts that live and die by their brands but that is far from most people. I think of myself and others when trying to understand how consumers buy a company's products and/or services.

All companies can be affected by trends to some degree. However, I tend to prefer companies that are less subject to trends like Home Depot (HD), Walmart (WMT), The Procter & Gamble Company (PG), International Paper Company (IP), and the Kraft-Heinz Company (KHC). Sure, all of these companies may be affected by changing consumer trends and tastes, but their product/services are more focused and lean further towards the baseline needs of consumers as opposed to their wants.

One year a consumer may buy a pair of Nike tennis shoes and then for the next two years not buy any products from the Nike brand at all. Maybe a consumer will purchase Reebok or New Balance shoes in the following years instead. The clothing and shoe industry are constantly subject to trends because it's a consumer market based more heavily on the wants of consumers as opposed to their basic baseline needs. Perhaps Puma will release a new shoe one year that is the next craze in style and comfort, this in turn will affect Nike's future revenue figures negatively. A decrease in Nike's revenue will likely be reflected by a decrease in stock price when the quarterly report is released, and investors react negatively to it.

Another reason I don't currently see Nike (NKE) stock as a good investment despite strong sales figures and a great looking upwards stock chart; is the P/E ratio of the stock. Currently as I write this section of the book in August 2018, the P/E ratio is 68. A P/E ratio of 68 is far too high to consider this stock a bargain. My general rule when choosing a blue-chip company to invest in is; the P/E ratio is to be 30 and below (unless I expect the company to deliver high growth in the future). A P/E ratio of 68 indicates the stock is priced for growth. Investors are willing to pay more for a share of stock in relation to the earnings per share (EPS); expecting growth in the future.

Even though Nike (NKE) may have more potential markets to expand into and an ever-growing population of potential customers over the future years, I still do not consider it a strong investment at the current valuation. I see Nike growing as a brand in future years, but I would not say the growth would be rapid enough to warrant making an investment at a P/E ratio of 68. When I buy a stock, I look for a bargain; if not a bargain at least a reasonably priced stock (based on P/E ratio) where there is room for recovery if a downward price correction or an overreaction among investors occurs.

A significant drop in share price in a high P/E ratio stock may still not present a good investment opportunity considering how overvalued the stock was in the first place. Meaning a 10% drop in share price in a company with a P/E ratio of 100 is not presenting as good an opportunity as a 10% drop in a company with a P/E of 22; assuming all other factors are in place to warrant a possible investment (strong revenues, good profit margins, competitive advantage, etc.).

If a company is subject to trends based on consumer desires or wants it doesn't mean the stock will never present a good investment opportunity. Sometimes the market can misprice and overlook a stock based on an overall negative perception of a stock and its performance. This may lead to the stock being undervalued based on key fundamentals like the P/E ratio, revenues, gross profit, net income, assets, and cash on hand. Also, an overreaction may take place by shareholders like we talked about in the Facebook (FB) example, that can be taken advantage of. Be wary of companies affected by trends but never right them off by any means.

However, as I mentioned previously, companies like Facebook (FB), Netflix (NFLX), Tesla (TSLA) and other technology-based companies with business models based more on wants/desires of consumers are a different story. Technology based blue-chip companies are always in the spot light ("hot stocks") and are popular with a large amount of "crazy" and irrational investors. Irrational investors often make irrational trading decisions which often lead to investment opportunities for the rational investor.

Movement in a company's share price is largely based on investor perception and sentiment surrounding a company and its stock. Meaning, how investors feel about a company in general. Investor perception alone can often move a stock in price with almost no fundamental investment strategy behind it. We will cover the concept of investor perception in further reading.

Remember when an investor buys a stock they are buying a small piece of a company/business. This is the basis of publicly traded companies; they are basically owned by the public or the shareholders of the stock. This is a crucial point many investors overlook when buying stock in a company. You want to buy into a business that is not over priced and one that is profitable. The goal for any business is to make money and grow over time. Your goal as an investor is to get the best possible deal when purchasing shares in relation to the strength, future growth, and profitability of a company. If you see a company with a high P/E ratio and invest, you are probably overpaying for your shares in most instances. By purchasing shares at bargain values, we give ourselves a good margin of safety.

Chapter 18: Reading the Income Statement

To become a successful investor, you must be able to read an income statement for a given company. There are three main sections of a company's income statement we must pay attention to.

Income Statement

1. Revenue or Net sales = Revenue is the income that a business has from its regular business activities, usually from the sale of goods and/or services to customers. Revenue is also referred to as sales or turnover. "Revenue." *Wikipedia*. Wikimedia Foundation Inc, 26 Sept 2018. Web. 13 Sept 2018. https://en.wikipedia.org/wiki/Revenue

2. Gross Profit = Revenue – Cost of Goods Sold (COGS). Gross profit is the profit a company makes after deducting the costs associated with making and selling its products, or the costs associated with providing its services. Or in other words, the difference between revenue and the cost of making a product or providing a service, before deducting overheads, payroll, taxation, interest payments and other expenses.

Note: It is very important that a company has a positive gross profit. A positive gross profit shows that a company can make money on their goods/ services sold before other expenses are taken into account. If a company is not able to achieve a positive gross profit, that is usually not a good sign for a company because making its products /services is costing the company more than the products or services sell for.

3. Net Income (NI) = Is calculated by subtracting total expenses from total revenues. So, this is our revenue minus everything else; cost of goods sold (COGS), selling expenses, general and administrative expenses, overheads, payroll, taxation, interest, and all other expenses. Net income is the earnings of a company before dividends are subtracted.

Net income is referred to as the bottom-line. It is very important to us as investors because we use the net income to calculate Earnings Per Share (EPS) for a company, which we in turn use to calculate our Price/Earnings Ratio (P/E).

Chapter 19: Reading the Balance Sheet

To become a successful investor, you must also be able to read a balance sheet for a company. There are three main sections of a company's balance sheet we must pay attention to.

Balance Sheet

1. Assets

"All assets should be divided into current and noncurrent assets. An asset is considered current if it can reasonably be converted into cash within one year. Cash, inventories and net receivables are all important current assets because they offer flexibility and solvency for a company." Ross, Sean. "What items on the balance sheet are most important in fundamental analysis?." *Investopedia*. Investopedia, LLC., Web. 18 Sept 2018. https://www.investopedia.com/ask/answers/050615/what-items-balance-sheet-are-most-important-fundamental-analysis.asp

Cash is of great importance – "Companies that generate a lot of cash are often doing a good job satisfying customers and getting paid. In contrast, too much cash can be worrisome, too little can raise a lot of red flags." Ross, Sean. "What items on the balance sheet are most important in fundamental analysis?." *Investopedia*. Investopedia, LLC., Web. 18 Sept 2018. https://www.investopedia.com/ask/answers/050615/what-items-balance-sheet-are-most-important-fundamental-analysis.asp

So, under the Assets section of a company's balance sheet we focus on three main areas.

1. Current Assets (A and B)

A. Cash or Cash Equivalents:

 This shows us how much cash a company has.

B. Total Current Assets:

An asset is considered current if it can reasonably be converted into cash within one year. Total current assets take into account: cash or cash equivalents, short term investments, net receivables, inventory, and other current assets.

Remember: An asset is considered current if it can reasonably be converted into cash within one year. This is good for solvency and generating a healthy cash flow into the company; which keeps a company operational on a day to day basis.

C. Total Assets:

This is the bottom line of the assets section on the balance sheet; it shows us the total assets a company has. Total assets take into account everything under current assets - plus long-term investments, property plant and equipment, goodwill, intangible assets, accumulated amortization, other assets, and deferred long-term asset charges.

Note: This is the bottom line of the asset section on the balance sheet of a company. We use this total when comparing a company's total assets vs. total liabilities.

2. Liabilities

Like assets, liabilities are either current or noncurrent. Current liabilities are obligations due within a year. Fundamental investors look for companies with fewer liabilities than assets.

Ross, Sean. "What items on the balance sheet are most important in fundamental analysis?." *Investopedia*. Investopedia, LLC., Web. 18 Sept 2018. https://www.investopedia.com/ask/answers/050615/what-items-balance-sheet-are-most-important-fundamental-analysis.asp

Primarily under the liabilities section we look at two main sections.

A. Total Current Liabilities:

The items in this section include accounts payable, short/current long-term debt, and other current liabilities.

B. Total Liabilities:

Total liabilities are always displayed on the balance sheet and represent the total debt of an entity. Items in this section include all items found under total current liabilities plus long-term debt, other liabilities, deferred long-term liability charges, minority interest, and negative goodwill.

3. Equity

Equity = assets − (minus) liabilities. Equity represents how much the company's shareholders actually have claim to. This is represented as a number referred to as Net Tangible Assets on the bottom of a company's balance sheet. Net tangible assets are a company's total assets subtracting both intangible assets (such as goodwill and intellectual property) and total liabilities. As investors we always want to see a positive number for the net tangible assets.

Chapter 20: The P/E Ratio and Earnings Per Share (EPS)

Let's talk more in depth about the P/E ratio. The P/E ratio stands for Price/Earnings ratio. The P/E ratio is one of the most important tools in identifying a stock on a value basis; it's a good indicator on how a stock is priced or valued (cheaply, reasonably, or overpriced). Now let's get into what it ultimately means to you the investor. The P/E ratio for a given company measures the share price relative to the company's earnings-per share (EPS). Or in other words market value per share vs. earnings per share. So, how does this work and how is it calculated.

To begin we will use a fictional company to illustrate how the P/E ratio is calculated. You have been doing some research and found Company ABC. Company ABC sells building materials; nails, screws, tools, drywall etc. Think of it as a competitor to Home Depot (HD). You have been looking at the stock and considering investing in the company. Now it's time for you to look at and evaluate the P/E ratio. Company ABC is currently trading for $55 per share.

Here's how P/E ratio works and is calculated. Let's say Company ABC ends the year with a net income of $20 billion. Company ABC has a total of 2.5 billion outstanding shares (the number of shares distributed between all investors). Every publicly traded company in the stock market has a certain number of shares. Some companies can issue more shares (stock offering) or sometimes they can buy back some shares (share buyback); that is a separate topic. Generally, companies have a set number of outstanding shares.

So, back to Company ABC with a yearly net income of $20 billion and 2.5 billion outstanding shares. P/E ratio = market value per share (the price you see on the computer screen) / earnings per share (EPS). So, let's calculate the latter; the earnings per share (EPS) based on our example. So, $20 billion in income / 2.5 billion outstanding shares = $8. You have just calculated the earnings per share (EPS) for Company ABC to be $8. For every outstanding share, Company ABC makes $8 in income.

Earnings per share (EPS) is largely regarded as one of the most important factors in determining a company's individual share price because it tells investors how much money the company makes on a per share basis. By dividing a company's share price by its earnings per share (EPS), an investor can determine the fair market value of a stock in terms of what the market is willing to pay for it (in terms of a price multiple, the numerical value of the P/E ratio) based on a company's current earnings.

Now, let's plug that into our equation and finally determine the P/E ratio of Company ABC. So, this is how it's done:

$55 Price (P) / $8 Earnings Per Share (E) = 6.875. So, the P/E ratio of Company ABC is 6.875.

Keep in mind that the net income (NI) of a company is subject to change over time as quarterly reports are released every three months (which influences the P/E ratio). Also, as the share price moves up and down the P/E ratio also changes. Lower earnings per share (EPS) values can significantly increase the P/E ratio which will in turn present less of a bargain on the shares based on a higher P/E ratio.

The lower the "E" value in relation to the "P" value in the P/E equation, the higher the P/E ratio will be. In contrast, the higher the "E" value in relation to the "P" value in the P/E equation, the lower the P/E ratio will be.

Company ABC: EPS = $8 and P/E = 6.875

This is a rather low P/E ratio (P/E of 6.875 from our above example), which means shares are priced/valued rather cheaply. A P/E of 6.875 usually indicates that a company is undervalued and is presenting a good bargain on its shares considering the company's other fundamentals are strong; stable and/or rising revenues, healthy profit margins, assets greater then liabilities, and a substantial amount of cash on hand.

The P/E ratio is sometimes referred to as the price multiple. It is referred to as the price multiple because the P/E ratio shows how much (in terms of multiples) an investor is willing to pay per dollar of company earnings (EPS) for a single share of the company. In the case of Company ABC, an investor is willing to pay 6.875 times the EPS for a single share of Company ABC. So, this means an investor pays $6.875 for every $1 of the current earnings per share EPS in Company ABC.

Example break down:

Company ABC, current share price = $55

Company ABC, earnings per share (EPS) = $8

Company ABC, P/E (or the price multiple) = 6.875

So, 6.875 x $8 = $55 (share price the investor is willing to pay)

We just came full circle and determined the share price of Company ABC, which is $55 per share.

It is important to understand that the P/E ratio should not be the only determining factor an investor looks at when purchasing shares of a company. The earnings per share (EPS) and the P/E ratio for a company may appear to be presenting a good value, but a company may have a significant amount of debt and other liabilities. A large amount of debt would not show in the P/E ratio but may signal that a company is in trouble and is not financially sound. Always look at the income statement and balance sheet of a company and do not use the P/E ratio as the sole variable to determine the viability of an investment.

Chapter 21: eBay – Business Model

Let's put what we have learned so far into practice and talk about a current opportunity I see in the stock market. I'm writing this chapter on 8/15/2018 and I will make a prediction on a stock I currently have on my radar and see as possibly a good investment opportunity. You will see how I strategically analyze the stock and you have the pleasure of seeing if my prediction will be correct in the future.

Currently a company I see opportunity in is eBay (EBAY). Previously I mentioned Nike (NKE) as a company that can be affected by trends and how a significant part of its business is based on the wants as opposed to the baseline needs of its customers. One of the main reasons I like eBay (EBAY) as a company is, it has a business model that is rather resilient to trends and is heavily based on needs of its users; as opposed to their wants. Not being strongly affected by these factors makes a company more durable and predictable to me. One of the best risk management tactics is to invest in companies that are less likely to be affected by trends and wants of consumers in a negative way. Companies that rely heavily on the needs of people provide investors with greater stability over the long run.

This is not to be confused with a company that perhaps releases a new technology product which becomes very trendy and popular thus increasing revenues in a company. Or perhaps an emerging biofuel company that has great potential in the future. The strategy that I discuss here applies to established companies and looks at their core business from a stability perspective in years to come.

Let's assume you want to sell a microscope that has been in your garage for the last five years. You have numerous platforms these days where you can post your microscope up for sale. You can use Facebook, Craigslist, Let Go, and eBay – among others. With the eBay platform you also have a variety of selling options for your microscope. For instance, you can't auction your item on these other platforms, but you can on eBay. Also, there are really no shipping options for items/products on these other platforms.

eBay offers many ways you can sell and ship a product. Also, eBay offers refunds to buyers if they are not satisfied under certain conditions. You can sell your item in an auction scenario, a "buy it now sale", set a reserve price, and other options that the other platforms do not offer. Buyers also have a variety of payment options on eBay like PayPal and debit/credit cards. eBay also reaches an international audience as opposed to the other platforms catering to more localized transactions between sellers and buyers. The bottom line is, eBay is a great and established platform to sell a variety of merchandise on.

Most people these days sell their items using multiple platforms to create greater exposure and increase their market size. Does the option for people to sell products via other platforms present eBay with competition in its sector? Absolutely. But I look at eBay as one of the dominant if not the most dominant platforms to sell any kind of item on. Something like Craigslist does not have a category for scientific equipment; but eBay does. So, as I look at a company like eBay I see some competition but not any significant enough at the moment to lower company revenues significantly and affect the company adversely in years to come. So, this is one check I can put on my check list of criteria for the company as a potential investment.

Earlier I mentioned that eBay is less prone to be affected by trends and has a business model based largely on the needs of its users. Let's look at eBay's business model for further understanding. eBay primarily makes money from sellers on its platform; the company makes a certain percentage of the total amount of a sale for every listing. It also makes money by charging for larger pictures and some other extra descriptive information. For sellers on the platform, the first 50 item listings are free. After that, eBay charges some amount for every additional listing. eBay also makes a very good chunk of money from PayPal (transaction fees) and eBay Enterprise (an eBay company that helps brick and mortar retailers create online shopping sites for their brands). Phillips, Jack. "How does eBay make money?." *Quora*. Quora, 21 Feb 2017. Web. 15 Aug 2018. https://www.quora.com/How-does-eBay-make-money

I like this business model because eBay makes money from other peoples' items and transaction fees. eBay does not need to create and manufacture a product(s) and sell it in the market; which can be costly in development, face high competition, and carry high risk. Their business model is not capital intensive.

Consumers that are buying items from eBay may be buying items for their wants or needs; probably skewed heavier toward wants. However, the sellers on eBay are usually selling things for need purposes. Meaning, someone needs to sell a car or a kitchen table that they no longer want or need but need to recover money for the particular item. Also, eBay is often used as a second income these days for people selling items online. So, the business model is based strongly on the needs of its users (the sellers) which makes a company less prone to trends. The process I will use for looking at eBay through fundamental/technical analysis in the coming chapter is not a standalone strategy for this particular company and it can be applied across the board when considering other companies and their stock.

Chapter 22: eBay – Fundamental and Technical Analysis

I will discuss eBay stock on a real time basis as I observe the stock myself. Today is 8/15/2018 and I'm looking at the eBay stock chart. The current stock price is $33.76 per share. I expand the stock chart on the Yahoo Finance platform to a 5-day chart and see that on 8/14/2018 the stock hit an intraday high of $34.73 per share. At this point I'm not doing anything special; but rather simply going through the stock chart.

Now I decide to click on a 1-year chart for eBay. I can quickly see that the current price of $33.76 per share on 8/15/2018 is basically the stock's one year low. I look at my stock app that shows me a concrete value for the 52-week low price; I confirm the 52-week low to be $32.85 per share.

Note: The 52-week high and 52-week low refers to the highest and lowest market prices of a given stock over a 52-week (one year) period.

So, now I know the current price of the stock is very close to its 52-week low. My stock app also tells me the 52-week high was $46.99 per share. A quick calculation shows me the percentage difference between the 52-week high and the current stock price of $33.76 per share (on 8/15/2018) is approximately 28%; a huge decline.

After this calculation I immediately see a possible investment opportunity. However, I need to perform further research to validate a possible investment and investigate why the large drop in share price has occurred. Through a simple web search, I now look at the company's quarterly/ yearly revenues, gross profits, net income (NI), and earnings per share (EPS).

Revenue: (EBAY)

The annual revenues (net sales) for (EBAY) are as follows:

2013: $16.05 Billion

2014: $17.90 Billion

2015: $8.59 Billion

2016: $8.98 Billion

2017: $9.57 Billion

"eBay Revenue, Profits – EBAY Annual Income Statement." *amigobulls.com*. Amigobulls, 15 August 2018. Web. 15 Aug 2018. https://amigobulls.com/stocks/EBAY/income-statement/annual

The quarterly revenues (net sales) in 2018 for (EBAY) are as follows:

March 31, 2018: $2.58 Billion (Quarter 1)

June 30, 2018: $2.64 Billion (Quarter 2)

"eBay Revenue, Profits – EBAY Quarterly Income Statement." *amigobulls.com*. Amigobulls, 15 August 2018. Web. 15 Aug 2018. https://amigobulls.com/stocks/EBAY/income-statement/quarterly

Next, we will take a look at gross profits (revenue – cost of goods = gross profit) to see how much money the company makes on their sales. Gross profit is the profit a company makes after deducting the costs of making and selling its products, or the costs of providing its services; before deducting overheads, payroll, taxation, interest payments and other expenses.

Gross Profit: (EBAY)

The annual gross profits of (EBAY) are as follows:

2013: $11.01 Billion

2014: $12.17 Billion

2015: $6.82 Billion

2016: $6.97 Billion

2017: $7.35 Billion

"eBay Revenue, Profits – EBAY Annual Income Statement." *amigobulls.com*. Amigobulls, 15 August 2018. Web. 15 Aug 2018. https://amigobulls.com/stocks/EBAY/income-statement/annual

The quarterly gross profits in 2018 for (EBAY) are as follows:

March 31, 2018: $2.02 Billion (Quarter 1)

June 30, 2018: $2.04 Billion (Quarter 2)

"eBay Revenue, Profits – EBAY Quarterly Income Statement." *amigobulls.com*. Amigobulls, 15 August 2018. Web. 15 Aug 2018. https://amigobulls.com/stocks/EBAY/income-statement/quarterly

Now, let's analyze the data we have in front of us so far. We can see that after 2014 revenues and gross profits decreased significantly. However, revenues and gross profits have increased from 2015 through 2017; two consecutive years. Also, we can look at the most recent revenue and gross profit figures from the latest two quarters in 2018 and see that there has been an increase in the second quarter of 2018 versus the first quarter of 2018 (for both revenue and gross profit).

Now, as investors we sometimes must look a little into the future and form a calculated hypothesis on a possible investment. If we take the average of the revenues in the first two quarters of 2018 we would get $2.61 billion. So, if we were to extrapolate that average of $2.61 billion per quarter for the remaining two quarters in 2018, the yearly revenue for 2018 would be $10.44 billion. Ending 2018 with an annual revenue (estimated) of $10.44 billion would mean that eBay's yearly revenue has increased for three consecutive years (2015-2018). Increasing revenue in a company is a sign of growth; which is always good for the investor.

Earlier we had gone through eBay's business model and talked about the strengths I see in the business as a whole. Now, I can concretely see that over the last two consecutive years revenue has increased and probably will increase for a 3rd consecutive year at the end of 2018.

From the data we can also see that eBay makes a healthy gross profit on its sales. A positive gross profit is the first sign that a company is on the right path to profitability. Sometimes you will come across companies with a negative gross profit; meaning their cost of goods sold (COGS) is more than their revenue (net sales). A negative gross profit usually signals a company is in serious trouble.

Now, let's look at eBay's net income (NI). Remember: Net income (NI) is calculated by subtracting total expenses from total revenues. So, this is revenue minus everything else; cost of goods sold (COGS), selling expenses, general and administrative expenses, overheads, payroll, taxation, interest, and all other expenses. Net income is the earnings of the company before dividends are subtracted.

Net income (NI) is referred to as the bottom-line. It is very important to us as investors because we use the net income to calculate Earnings Per Share (EPS) for a company, which we in turn use to calculate our Price/Earnings Ratio (P/E). Net income is the money a company has left after all expenses are subtracted from revenues. As investors we always want to see a positive net income.

Net Income (NI): (EBAY)

2013: $2.86 Billion

2014: $46 Million

2015: $1.73 Billion

2016: $7.27 Billion

2017: $-1.02 Billion (Negative Income)

"eBay Revenue, Profits – EBAY Annual Income Statement." *amigobulls.com*. Amigobulls, 15 August 2018. Web. 15 Aug 2018. https://amigobulls.com/stocks/EBAY/income-statement/annual

The quarterly net income (NI) in 2018 for (EBAY) is as follows:

March 31, 2018: $407 Million (Quarter 1)

June 30, 2018: $642 Million (Quarter 2)

"eBay Revenue, Profits – EBAY Quarterly Income Statement." *amigobulls.com*. Amigobulls, 15 August 2018. Web. 15 Aug 2018. https://amigobulls.com/stocks/EBAY/income-statement/quarterly

From the above data we can see that the net income (NI) of eBay has being rather unsteady over the years. This is mostly due to varying expenses the company was obligated to pay over the years including significant tax payments. However, it is crucial to understand that these expenses are not related to the cost of goods sold (COGS). Sometimes a company will have varying expenses/obligations that are not directly related to the cost associated with producing its products/services; these "other" expenses can sometimes lead to a negative net income (NI).

However, we can see another trend from the data we have; net income has increased from quarter one (Q1) of 2018 to quarter two (Q2) of 2018. Improving financials are always a good sign and are indictive of company's overall health and future.

Now, let's look at the company's earnings per share (EPS).

Earnings Per Share (EPS): (EBAY)

The annual earnings per share (EPS) of (EBAY) are as follows:

2013: 2.18 EPS

2014: - 0.03 EPS (Negative EPS)

2015: 1.42 EPS

2016: 6.35 EPS

2017: - 0.95 EPS (Negative EPS)

"eBay Revenue, Profits – EBAY Annual Income Statement." *amigobulls.com*. Amigobulls, 15 August 2018. Web. 15 Aug 2018. https://amigobulls.com/stocks/EBAY/income-statement/annual

The quarterly EPS in 2018 for (EBAY) are as follows:

March 31, 2018: 0.40 EPS (Quarter 1)

June 30, 2018: 0.64 EPS (Quarter 2)

eBay Revenue, Profits – EBAY Quarterly Income Statement." *amigobulls.com*. Amigobulls, 15 August 2018. Web. 15 Aug 2018. https://amigobulls.com/stocks/EBAY/income-statement/quarterly

Again, the EPS for eBay has not been steady over the years; however, we can see an increase in EPS from Q1 of 2018 to Q2 of 2018 (a positive signal). Now, I will take a quick look at the balance sheet for eBay to see how much cash the company has. As of Q2 of 2018; the company has $1.64 billion in cash.

Now, I want to look at (EBAY) from an asset vs. liability standpoint. Remember, as we mentioned earlier we want a company to have greater assets than liabilities. The latest data from the balance sheet shows the following as of the latest quarter in 2018 (Q2):

Total assets: $23.99 Billion

Total liabilities: $16.84 Billion

eBay Balance Sheet – Quarterly (NASDAQ: EBAY)." *amigobulls.com*. Amigobulls, 15 August 2018. Web. 15 Aug 2018. https://amigobulls.com/stocks/EBAY/balance-sheet/quarterly

This data is another positive sign for the company. It is always good for a company's assets to be greater than its liabilities.

Now, that I have looked at the company from a business and operational perspective; I must now look at eBay and its share price from a value and bargain hunter standpoint. To look at the value a stock is presenting we must look at the P/E ratio. I see that the current P/E ratio of eBay is 6.45. This is a rather low P/E ratio which indicates that shares of eBay are selling at a bargain price.

Finally, to warrant any investment we have to round up all the conclusions we have come to about eBay (EBAY); and make a calculated investment decision:

1. A strong and established company that has proven itself over time. A household name that comes to mind when selling or buying items.

2. Stock price is near a 52-week low, despite rising revenues for two consecutive years.

3. Business model focused on the needs of its users; business not highly prone to trends.

4. Business model is not capital intensive, meaning eBay makes money on a percentage of each sale made and transaction fees. No products and product development required.

5. Revenue has increased from Q1 to Q2 of 2018, which will likely lead to an increase in revenue for the third consecutive year (estimated).

6. Company has had a positive gross profit for many years.

7. Net income (NI) and earnings per share (EPS) are positive (for Q1 and Q2 of 2018) and have increased from Q1 to Q2 of 2018; with an expectation to increase in the following quarters (estimated).

8. A low P/E ratio of 6.45 indicates the stock is selling at a value or bargain price.

9. $1.64 billion in cash as of Q2 2018.

10. Total assets are greater than total liabilities (this is a good sign).

Now, before an investor buys a stock there must be a clear goal set for the investment. Without a goal an investor has no exit strategy. So, below I will set a goal for myself on eBay (EBAY) as an investment.

Goal: 8-12% gain, within a 1 to 5-month time frame.

Based on this information I decide to purchase the stock. My buy order is executed at $33.80 per share - for 100 shares on 8/15/2018.

Chapter 23: Building an Investment Portfolio (Part 1)

So far, we have talked about well-established blue-chip companies with multibillion-dollar market capitalizations. We will now discuss how to build your investment portfolio based largely around these blue-chip companies. Later, we will expand into how you can introduce some smaller high growth companies into your portfolio and dividend paying stocks.

Building a strong investment portfolio is essentially all about risk management and capital allocation (how you divide your money up between different investments and investment types). Meaning that you have multiple well picked stocks and all your eggs are not in one basket. If you have $20,000 and you put it all in Walmart (WMT) stock, you would not be managing risk very well. Sure, Walmart (WMT) is a solid company but the financial markets can sometimes be unpredictable and experience significant corrections. Individual companies, even reputable ones can experience turbulent times. The way we manage unpredictability is through diversification and smart capital allocation (distribution).

When building an investment portfolio, it would not be very wise to open positions in Ford (F), General Motors (GM), and Toyota Motor Corp (TM) as your entire portfolio. Why? Well, even though you may consider these companies as well-run and established companies you would be putting all your eggs in one basket. Remember, success in the stock market is all about managing your risk and exposure.

Think of yourself as a hedge fund manager. Say your client comes in and asks you which stocks you have invested his hard-earned retirement money in. If you tell your client that you have divided his $2,000,000 between three automotive stocks; I can assure you if he knows anything at all about investing you probably won't be his money manager for too much longer. It doesn't take a genius to understand that putting all your eggs in one basket is not a good idea. Even though these are three different companies, they belong to the same automotive sector. So, if the automotive sector is affected adversely the entire portfolio may be in trouble and under-perform for a significant time frame.

Let's say one day you are watching the news and you see a new government bill being passed requiring U.S car manufacturers to offer six standard airbags, a lane departure warning system, and an average gas mileage figure of 42 mpg for their non-commercial vehicles starting with the 2023 model year. Usually news like this will have a negative effect on the prices of automotive stocks. Why? Well because now car manufacturers will have to invest more capital into their cars (research and development, assembly line adjustments etc.); possibly affecting upcoming quarterly profit margins and subsequently earnings per share (EPS). Short term investor outlook can be negative when news like this comes out, driving the stock prices down. Remember, a large portion of investors are quick to react to news which can affect stock prices significantly.

A company investing money into their products may be good in the long-run but in the short term it would probably eat into the company's profit margin. This negative effect on the profit margin could affect the stock prices in a negative way when quarterly earnings are released. So, if you had invested all your client's money into three automotive stocks and news like that came out, you would probably have some serious explaining to do on why all the positions are down. This is why it is smart to diversify your stock portfolio into different sectors. Always keep in mind that the first objective for any investor is to be a good risk manager and preserve the original capital invested.

So, how does an investor build a strong and diversified portfolio that manages risk? The beginning goal is not to be necessarily searching for new companies but rather to start brainstorming a list of companies that you are already familiar with. Remember, we are thinking of blue-chip companies. Think of names and brands you know; what comes to mind?

For me it's, Walmart, Home Depot, McDonalds, Ford, General Motors, IBM, Microsoft, Facebook, Kraft-Heinz, Coca-Cola, Amazon, AMD, eBay, Apple and many more. Just by thinking of some of the items in your household or establishments you frequent, you will inevitably come up with a list of some major companies. Most of these companies are the top performers in their respective sectors. When picking stocks to invest in, it is wise to invest in companies across different sectors. Of course, you can have multiple positions in the same sector (automotive, technology, biofuels etc.) if the stocks are presenting a good value, but in relation to the rest of your portfolio no sector should be greatly dominant.

By picking established companies that have proven themselves over decades you are performing risk management. Simply because many of these companies have performed well for generations and probably will keep performing and delivering for many more decades. This is why I strongly believe in investing in blue-chip companies as part of a good investment strategy. My general rule is, 40-60% of your investment portfolio should be comprised of blue-chip investments. The other 40-60% of your investment portfolio should be divided between dividend stocks, high-growth companies, and cash.

Chapter 24: Quantity, Probability, and Familiarization

Let's talk about having probability on your side as an investor. Personally, on my phone stock app I have approximately 60 stocks that I constantly observe. From time to time I may add a stock or delete one that I'm no longer interested in, but the list essentially remains 90% unchanged over time. Why? Well part of my investment strategy is by having a significant number of well-diversified companies on my stock app, I have a higher probability of being presented with an opportunity.

I have carefully picked these stocks and believe that they have a strong chance of presenting investment opportunities occasionally. The companies on my watch list vary in size (by market capitalization) and sector. However, from a fundamentals standpoint I believe they will present investment opportunities in time for various reasons. Also, by keeping my watchlist of stocks essentially unchanged I can become an expert on each company and its stock.

Let's assume you only had three stocks the you were looking at; International Business Machines (IBM), Ford (F), and Apple (AAPL). With only three stocks on your radar how often do you think you would be presented with a genuinely worthy investment opportunity? What about if you had the stocks of 20 big companies on your stock app which you looked at daily and searched for opportunities? Think about that for a while and I'm sure you will come to the correct conclusion that you need quantity and probability on your side. By no means am I suggesting that you should have 200 stocks at any given point on your watch list. But, have 20-30 strong and established companies, with an additional three to five riskier companies that have great promise in the future - under constant observation.

The beauty is, you will inevitably become very familiar with the companies on your watchlist. You will begin to see emerging patterns and develop a general sense of price action in each stock. This is exactly what you want as an investor; familiarization with a company is one of the strongest tools you can possess as an investor. You want to become an expert in the stocks on your watchlist. In the beginning stages of investing, you will have to look deep into the fundamentals of each company on your watchlist.

You will read many articles and news that has previously been written about the company and its stock. The initial stages of company analysis can be an intense process. However, as you become an expert in the companies on your watch list, you will only have to keep up with the latest news about the company or general market conditions. You can correlate the latest news with the information you already know about the company. Bottom line is, pick a well-diversified group of companies and become an expert in each one, this will give you an edge over the average investor that buys mostly on speculation – not fundamental analysis.

Chapter 25: The Baseball Analogy

Let's use a baseball analogy to demonstrate a point in the stock market. This analogy has been used for many decades within the investing world. When a player steps up to bat in baseball they only have three chances to hit the pitchers' ball before they strike out. The player also has a limited amount of time to bat; the batter can't stand on the hitting plate forever. The two big factors working against the players' favor of hitting a great ball is a limited number of chances to strike the ball and a limited amount of time to perform in. The batters' risk is rather high considering they have a maximum of three pitches to execute on and a very limited amount of time to execute in. Now, let's apply that to the stock market and look at our chances of hitting a homerun.

In the stock market we will think of the ball as a stock an investor wants to potentially buy or take a swing at. The swing is the decision to buy the stock. Every time the batter swings they are taking a chance or a risk. Every time an investor buys a stock they are also taking a risk. The batter or the investor don't know with 100% certainty if their swing or investment will be successful. However, the beautiful thing about the stock market is that as investors we have an unlimited amount of stocks to swing at and no specific time fame to make our investments in. Until we spot a good opportunity we don't have to take a swing or buy any stock. I sometimes give this example to people I introduce to stock market strategies because a lot of investors feel pressure to make investments quickly. Always keep in mind that time and variety are on your side in the stock market.

Chapter 26: Investing in an Emerging Company (HUYA)

So far, we have talked about investing in established blue-chip companies. Now, we will discuss how to invest in an emerging company. Let's take a look at HUYA Inc. (HUYA), the Chinese streaming company (I'm writing this section on 9/19/2018). This isn't a blue-chip company, but it does have a multibillion-dollar market capitalization; approximately a $5.22 billion market capitalization (as of 9/19/2018) - which is large but not a huge mega-cap stock like Home Depot (HD) with a market capitalization of around $225 billion. There is no textbook definition of what a blue-chip company is; but they are generally well known, large, and established companies. So far, we have covered investing in established domestic companies; now we will take a look at how to invest in an emerging company based in China.

HUYA is not a blue-chip company, so first of all how did I come across the company and its stock? I was reading through posts on a stock chat room when someone mentioned it, so I decided to do some research and look further into the company. Remember you can use these stock boards/chat rooms to your advantage to potentially generate new investment ideas.

HUYA Inc. (HUYA) is in the business of running live game streaming platforms in China. Its platforms allow broadcasters and viewers to interact during live streaming. The company also provides advertising and online game-related services. "As of December 31, 2017, its live streaming content covered approximately 2,600 games, including mobile, PC, and console games." "Company Overview of HUYA Inc.." *Bloomberg*. Bloomberg L.P., 24 Sept 2018. Web. 19 Sept,2018.
https://www.bloomberg.com/research/stocks/private/snapshot.asp?privcapId=431096194

HUYA is the biggest streaming company in China. HUYA had an IPO (Initial Public Offering) on May 10, 2018; basically, meaning the company became a publicly traded company on the New York Stock Exchange (NYSE).

I know that the Chinese market is growing very quickly and there is a lot of investment opportunity in China. Live streaming is incredibly popular, and China has a huge population of consumers and overall potential. I will now begin to go through a step by step analysis of this company to warrant a potential investment.

I will begin by looking at some stock charts for the company. By looking at a stock chart I can see that the HUYA stock had an all-time high price of $50.82 per share on 6/15/2018. The very latest closing price of the stock as of Wednesday 9/19/2018 is $25.64 per share. The first thing that strikes me is the huge difference between the all-time peak share price and the current price as of today. I will do a calculation to see the percent difference between the two prices.

$25.64 / $50.82 = .504 or approximately 50%

A 50% decline from the peak price on 6/15/2018 to the current closing price on 9/19/2018 is a huge difference; approximately a 50% drop over a 3-month period. Before, I start performing fundamental analysis on the company I want to expand the stock chart and do some technical analysis. Since the company recently had an IPO on May 10, 2018 there is only about four months of stock chart to look at. Looking at the stock chart a few pieces of information begin to stand out to me.

Technical analysis:

1. From the peak price of $50.82 per share on 6/15/2018 there was a steady decline to a share price of $28.40 per share on 7/6/2018 (with small fluctuations along the way but a general sharp down trend).

2. After reaching a low price of $28.40 per share on 7/6/2018, the stock began to steadily rise until 7/19/2018.

3. For three consecutive trading days; starting from July 17 through July 19 (inclusive), the stock price peaked each day around $40.00 per share. After July 19, HUYA stock began a gradual decline to the share price it is today.

Conclusions from technical analysis:

1. Usually IPO's have a lot of investment excitement around them. The peak price of $50.82 per share on 6/15/2018 came about one month after the IPO date; after a strong and steady rise in stock price.

2. After reaching the peak price the stock began to steadily decline for various reasons.

A) Profit taking by investors.

B) The stock had reached "over-bought" territory giving investors concerns with how much higher the stock could possibly go. Also, the stock had become overvalued from a fundamental standpoint.

C) Ongoing tariff talks between the U.S and China had investors in an uneasy state of mind.

3. The stock found support around $28 per share after its decline and then slowly rose back to around $40 per share because investor confidence, perception, and overall excitement around the stock was still high. Many investors believed that the stock could rise back to its peak price once again.

4. After hitting $40 per share the price began to decline again.

Before we move onto the fundamental analysis of HUYA we must understand a few things from a technical analysis and investor psychology standpoint that applies to stocks in general. There is currently a lot of excitement and hype around HUYA with investors; however, the company has not yet proven itself through steady performance and returns. This is where we have to slightly alter our investment mentality from the way we invest in blue-chip stocks to the way we approach companies that do not yet have a solid track record (new companies and most penny stocks).

"Good" hype or even good news in an unproven company tends to be very short lived; which reflects in quick spikes in share price which are only sustained for a short period of time. However, "bad" news for an unestablished company can send the stock price into free fall causing significantly lower stock prices, where they will remain for a prolonged period of time until good news comes out or investor perception begins to change.

The reason for this phenomenon is that investors still do not have enough confidence in the company behind the stock; so, gains are short lived (because investors believe the gains are unsustainable). In contrast, bad news can have a prolonged effect resulting in low share prices that will remain low for a significant period of time. Investors need to be reaffirmed with constant good news and financial data that the company has an upside and a strong future to build their confidence.

This is quite different then what tends to happen in blue-chip companies when news or results come out. Good news in blue-chip stocks tends to "last" for a significant time. The stock price may steadily go up for weeks or even months, because the general confidence and perception of the company is already high. On the contrary, "bad" news generally doesn't last too long in solid blue-chip companies unless it's a piece of news or a financial result that is significantly detrimental and would impact the company negatively for the long-term.

Earlier in the book we talked about how blue-chip companies tend to rebound very quickly from "bad" news which can often lead to great investment opportunities for us. This is because investors believe that these strong established companies can whether almost all situations and eventually will rebound from them. So, we have to look at established companies and new companies from different perspectives as investors. Now let's get back to HUYA and look at the company from a fundamental and growth view point.

On 8/13/2018 HUYA quarterly (Q2) results were announced, quarterly results were solid. Revenue and the number of paying users had gone up significantly compared to the previous quarter, but general forward guidance was "light" for the company. The CEO stated the revenue in the following quarter would continue to grow but not as fast as possibly expected by some analysts.

The big picture based on this information is that general investor perception of HUYA stock is still generally high. However, with constant tariff talks and a not so crystal-clear view of the future for the company, investor confidence has slowly faded reflecting in the lower stock price. However, investors are constantly keeping in mind that the stock was $40-50 per share at one point and many still believe that those share prices are attainable again. This will play into part of our investment strategy in this company. So far, we have four positives for investing in HUYA.

1. Growth of revenue and users from one quarter to another.

2. Investor psychology - Investors believing that the stock will once again reach its peak price per share or come close to it. So, if the stock price begins to slowly rise from its current levels, more investors could potentially jump on the band wagon believing that the stock is heading back toward its peak prices. This will increase the demand for the stock which will result in higher share prices.

3. A general conviction that the company will continue growing in the future for reasons like: China's huge population and new users discovering and using the HUYA streaming platform. The company is

still relatively new so there is plenty of potential for growth and adaptation of its services.

4. With time HUYA could potentially enter new fields and theoretically offer more services and new products; this could drive revenues higher in the future. For example, Google started as a search engine but now has expanded to offering products that range from laptops to mobile phones and has even entered the world of autonomous driving technology. (end of reason 4)

Next, I will do some research on the company's recent revenue figures. Since the company recently did an IPO (May 10th, 2018) there are limited financial results we can look at. The majority of these financial results are prior to HUYA going public but are still valid in terms of revenue and other financial details. Let's take a look at some financial data for the company.

The annual revenues (net sales) for (HUYA) are as follows:

2016: $119.95 Million

2017: $323.28 Million

"HUYA Inc. ADR." *MarketWatch*. MarketWatch Inc, 19 Sept 2018. Web. 19 Sept 2018.
https://www.marketwatch.com/investing/stock/huya/financials

The quarterly revenues (net sales) for (HUYA) are as follows (this is all the data that is currently available):

2017: $67.24 Million (Quarter 2)

2017: $87.48 Million (Quarter 3)

2017: $112.04 Million (Quarter 4)

2018: $132.66 Million (Quarter 1)

2018: $162.79 Million (Quarter 2)

"HUYA Inc. ADR." *MarketWatch*. MarketWatch Inc, 19 Sept 2018. Web. 19 Sept 2018.
https://www.marketwatch.com/investing/stock/huya/financials/income/quarter

From this data we can see that revenue in HUYA is growing rapidly. The revenue had more than doubled from 2016 to 2017 and has increased from Q1 to Q2 of 2018. The combined revenue for Q1+Q2 of

2018 is $295.45 million, almost as much as the total revenue in 2017, just in the first two quarters. This data shows us the company is growing.

By looking at further data, I can see that the company has had a positive gross profit for all its five most recent reported financial quarters. This lets me know that the COGS (cost of goods sold) is less than the revenue; which is good. You will see some companies where the COGS is actually higher than the revenue. In this case, HUYA takes in more revenue than it costs the company to offer its goods/services which is a positive sign. If you see a company that has consistent negative gross profits you should probably not invest in that company. It means that even before taxes, payroll, and other expenses are taken out (how we calculate net income); the company cannot even make a profit on their products or services offered.

Note: It is very important that a company has a positive gross profit. A positive gross profit shows that a company can make money on their goods/services sold before other expenses are considered. If a company is not able to achieve a positive gross profit, that is usually not a good sign for a company because making/offering its products/services is costing the company more than the products or services sell for.

Before I make my decision, I want to look at HUYA from a total asset vs. total liability standpoint. Remember, as we mentioned earlier we want a company to have more assets than liabilities. The latest data from the balance sheet shows the following as of the latest quarter in 2018 (Q2):

Total assets: $929.52 Million

Total liabilities: $147.63 Million

"HUYA Inc. ADR." *MarketWatch*. MarketWatch Inc, 19 Sept 2018. Web. 19 Sept 2018. https://www.marketwatch.com/investing/stock/huya/financials/balance-sheet/quarter

We can see that the assets are much higher than the liabilities which is another positive signal. Remember: Equity = assets – liabilities. Equity represents how much the company's shareholders actually have claim to. This is represented as a number referred to as Net Tangible Assets on the bottom of a company's balance sheet. Net tangible assets are a company's total assets subtracting both intangible assets (such as goodwill and intellectual property) and total liabilities. As investors we want to see a positive number for Net Tangible Assets.

Upon further research I can see that HUYA has posted a negative net income (NI) for most of its financial quarters. This would result in a P/E ratio of zero or a negative P/E ratio. Remember, the EPS (earnings per share) is calculated from the net income (NI). This means that a company with a negative net income would have "zero" or a negative value plugged into the "E" portion of the P/E ratio equation. You will often see no P/E value displayed for a company that generates a negative net income (this is the case for HUYA).

This does not worry me in this case for a few reasons. The company is still growing and as long as they can keep increasing revenues and their gross profit stays positive; I believe that the expenses that are contributing to a negative net income (NI) can be worked out over time. The company is still in the beginning stages so there could be a lot of money pouring into research and development (R&D) and general structuring of the company for the future.

To confirm this, I look at the income statement for HUYA. I can see that every quarter a significant amount of money ($10 - $20 million dollars per quarter) has been dedicated to research and development and SG&A - selling, general & administrative expenses. The expenses that are causing a negative net income are not directly related to the cost of producing/offering the company's services or products (cost of goods sold, COGS). Companies can often perform cost cutting measures related to their non-COGS related expenses.

Based on everything we have discussed I believe that there is a strong upside for an investment in HUYA. China has a huge population and even if HUYA can capture a percentage of that population as its market share the company should prosper. Their business in future years should not be very capital intensive (as opposed to something like a car company that has to build a car from scratch) and start generating a consistent positive net income. I strongly believe investor confidence will return to this stock which will be reflected by an increasing stock price. I decide to invest; my buy order is executed on 9/20/2018 at a price of $25.62 per share, for 150 shares.

Goal for investment:

PT (Price target): $40-50 per share within a 3-9-month period.

Strategy: Sell shares in lots of 50 shares as the investment becomes profitable to maximize gains (and lock in profits) if price moves further upwards.

Things to take into consideration when investing in a non-established company (most of these points also apply to established companies):

1. Is the company growing and/or have potential for future growth?

2. Does the company at least make a positive gross profit?

3. Does the company offer a product/service that is unique or proprietary; that is better than the competition? This will give a company a durable competitive advantage.

4. Do company insiders hold a significant number of shares? Usually, when insiders of a company hold significant positions within a company it signals that they have confidence in the performance of the company in the future.

5. Does the company have good management in place that has a good business sense and places strong value on shareholder satisfaction?

6. Does the company have assets that are greater than liabilities (this would be a good thing)?

7. Does the company have good cash flow? For example, a company may need to constantly raise cash (because the company may have a negative net income which hinders free cash flow into the company) to stay operational. They will finance themselves by issuing stock offerings and constantly diluting the shareholder.

8. Is the company in danger of a reverse stock split? Companies can perform reverse stock splits to stay compliant with NASDAQ listing rules. If a company closes below $1 per share for 30 consecutive days, the NASDAQ sends the company a written notice. Even though after a reverse stock split occurs the share price is adjusted on a post-split basis (to a higher price); there is a constant danger that if the company continues to underperform the share price will continue going down and now the investor also has less shares in total. After several reverse stock splits and underperformance by the company, an investment that was once sizeable could become almost worthless as the investor's number of shares is constantly decreased along with the sinking stock price. (end of #8)

Seeking out a company that is positioned for future growth can also be applied to established blue-chip companies. In these types of stocks your primary goal is to look for rising revenues year over year (YOY) and rising quarterly earnings (Q/Q). Of course, other fundamental data must be looked at like the P/E, EPS, gross profit, liabilities, assets, net income etc. Often times many blue-chips stocks can deliver strong growth and solid returns. I mention this because many investors believe that growth stocks are only associated with small or medium sized companies. There a plenty of growing blue-chip companies one can invest in.

Chapter 27: Selling Your Investments and Locking in Profits

Thus far we have talked about how to spot an opportunity in a stock and take advantage of it. So, let's change pace and talk about the best way to sell your stocks and maximize your profits. Let's assume you purchased $10,000 worth of stock in a technology company with stock symbol FICT (not an actual company just for the example). You bought the stock at a price of $25 per share after some in-depth research and company analysis. So, you are currently holding 400 shares of FICT. FICT hovers around your buy price for about a week but does not move significantly in either the up or down direction.

One morning you see that FICT stock has moved up 6%. Its only 11:30 AM and your stock is up 6% from your buy price of $25 per share, making the current price of FICT $26.50. Now, the novice investor may get excited and sell their entire position in the stock. So, that would mean that the investor has sold all 400 shares at a price of $26.50 per share giving them a cash total of $10,600 (a $600 profit).

However, selling your entire position sometimes is not the best decision especially if there is more upside potential in the stock. Professional investors usually never sell their entire position at once for a variety of reasons. One of the most important reasons is risk management. Even though your stock is up you sometimes can impose significant limitations on yourself by selling your entire position, by possibly limiting how much profit you could realize on the original investment. Suppose you go to lunch and come back to see that FICT share price is now at $27.85 per share. You would have missed out on more potential profit by selling the entire position at once.

Of course, we should never chase the maximum potential profit a stock can deliver, but sometimes when a stock shows promise to move significantly higher we can use a different strategy for exiting our position. Usually when a stock moves up and you think it has a good chance of continuing its upward movement you should only sell a certain percentage of your position ("scaling out" of the position). When you are up on a position it's always smart to sell and lock in profits (on a percentage of the total position) just in case the stock price drops significantly following its initial upward trend. As investors we often must make calculated decisions on how to best exit an investment; either by selling off the entire position or selling our position in percentage portions.

      Just like it is wise to "scale out" of a winning position, it is usually a good idea to "scale into" a new position. No investor can know with 100% certainty that a stock will go up in price. This is why it is first important to decide how much total capital you are willing to dedicate to a position and then invest in portions of that total amount. For example, if you decided to dedicate up to $10,000 to stock ABC, it is good risk management to enter the stock in $5,000 lots. This is not always necessary when making an investment, but it is good risk management practice. Always remember, anything you do in the stock market should be done with a huge emphasis on risk management. This is what separates "smart money" or the professional / institutional investor from "dumb money", the retail investor. Again, this is not said to degrade the retail investor, but rather give the retail investor a rubric for success.

Chapter 28: The Professional Investor

Most institutional and professional investors won't sell their entire position ("scaling out") during an uptrend for several reasons. Also, these kinds of investors usually enter a position by "scaling in" in portions. The main reasons behind these strategies are described below.

1) Liquidity:

Usually these kinds of investors deal with large quantities of shares and there simply could not be enough liquidity (meaning there is not enough volume to execute their sell order or buy order) in the stock to enter/exit their entire position swiftly and at the price they desire.

2) Trend Disruption when exiting a position:

When a large investor wants to exit a position they often don't want to "buck" the general trend if they are looking to maximize profits. If they sell their entire position an upward trend in stock price could be significantly disrupted and begin a downward trend. The selloff of large positions can often change the direction of a trend. So, typically an investor that is dealing with a large number of shares will sell their position in smaller portions that are not likely to affect the upward trend. They too are looking to maximize their profits, but they are smart enough to know that it is wise to lock in profits on a portion of a position. By not "upsetting" the upward trend, they position themselves to sell the remainder of their shares and maximize profits if the stock continues trending upward.

The same strategy can be applied when exiting a losing position. Often times large investors will exit a stock that's in decline in portions (unless it's a critical situation and they must get rid of all their shares very quickly). Their goal here is not to intensify the rate at which the stock is dropping in price by dumping a huge number of shares onto the market.

3) Stock Manipulation:

Sometimes a large investor will actually sell a portion of their shares not to lock in profits but to drive the stock price lower and pick up more shares at a cheaper price. This often happens when the large investor has a strong conviction that the stock is positioned to move higher in time. For example, John a hedge fund manager strongly believes a stock will move much higher when good quarterly earnings are reported in a few weeks' time. So, John the fund manager decides to sell a portion of his position to try to influence the share price to go down in order to buy up more shares and maximize his profit in a few weeks' time.

John sells 10,000 shares at $60.00 per share (a $600,000 position). The price of the stock begins to turn downwards as a large number of shares is unloaded on the market. In a few hours the stock has declined to $57.14 per share. The fund manager now decides to buy more shares with the $600,000 from the previous sale. So, $600,000 / $57.14 per share = 10,500 shares; John the fund manager has now gained an extra 500 shares. Large investors usually combine this strategy to drive prices lower by "setting off" stop-losses placed on the stock by many retail investors.

A stop-loss order is often used by an investor for a long position (when an investor is hoping the stock goes up in price). A stop-loss order will trigger a market order to sell when a stock trades below a certain price; the order is then executed at the next available price. Investors use stop-loss orders to limit their downside risk in case a stock begins to decline in price. Large investors can take advantage of stop-loss orders placed by retail investors.

For example, a large investor may know that there is a large cluster of stop-loss orders clustered around the $23-25 per share range for a particular stock. The large investor may sell a portion of their shares in order to drive the stock price lower so that these stop-loss orders are triggered, and a large number of shares will be sold. This will usually drive the share price even lower where the large investor wants to buy. The triggering of many stop-losses will also create the much-needed liquidity (a large volume of available shares) the large investor needs to do business and execute their large buy order quickly, efficiently, and at the price they desire.

Often times large investors looking to drive the price of a stock lower act when the market or sentiment around a stock is already low/weak. They understand that many retail investors panic easily and simply cannot afford to lose sizeable portions of their investment accounts if a stock were to go down in price significantly. When investors a very cautious about a stock going lower or general "shaky" market conditions are present, they will place stop-loss orders on their investments. In times of investor "weakness" is when these plans to drive a stock lower are generally executed for efficiency purposes by large investors.

4. Cost of doing business and staying under the radar:

Professional and institutional investors with large orders to execute usually "scale into" a position for the following reason. Large investors often want to stay under the "radar" when buying a stock. If a large investor wishes to enter a stock at a particular price point they will "scale into" their position in portions. If a large investor were to try to execute a large buy order at once, the demand for shares in the stock will go up drastically. So, part of their large order may be executed at their desired price, but as the stock begins to move higher due to the increased demand; the remaining portion of their buy order may not be executed at the desired point of entry or price per share. (end of reason #4)

Why is it important for you as the retail investor to know how the professionals execute their trades? Some of the strategies they use like "scaling into" and "scaling out" of their investments can also be implemented by the retail investor. Also, it is important to understand how the actions of large investors may influence the price of a stock.

Sometimes you may be stuck in a position for a long time and as soon as the stock goes a few points higher you instantly want to get out of the position and lock in your profits; this is understandable and sometimes the best course of action. However, if you have a strong case on why a stock could move considerably higher (for example a company releases great quarterly earnings) it's a good idea to sell your position in percentage portions. For example, you could sell 70 % of your shares to lock in the 6% profit (from our FICT example, Chapter 27) and then sell the remaining shares as the stock creeps higher. Remember being successful in the stock market is all about managing risk and implementing good timing. By selling a portion of your shares you are locking in profits and also minimizing your downside risk by only leaving 30% of the shares in the stock (you are essentially limiting your exposure in case the stock price begins to decline).

So far, we have talked about locking in profits, now let's discuss how to keep those profits for the long-term. Let's say you sold a position in a stock, that you had initially invested $20,000 in and you ended up making a 4% profit when you sold. So now you would have a total of $20,800 (a $800 profit) in your stock account assuming it was your only position. What's the next step and how do you make sure you hold onto the hard-earned profits you have made?

Chapter 29: Building an Investment Portfolio (Part 2)

I always tell investors that whenever they make a profit on an investment it is wise to put a percentage of the profit away as cash. Let's use the above example where an investor started with a $20,000 investment and now has a total account value of $20,800 after making a 4% profit. My formula is to put away 50% of your profits as cash into a non-investment related account(s). Meaning the investor would now have $20,400 for future investments. The reason I suggest putting away 50% of your profits is; as an investor you don't want to risk all the profit you made in future investments. Remember, after you have made a profitable trade no one can take the money away from you, except you by possibly making a bad investment decision. So, put 50% aside (into a savings/checking account or preferably into a CD account to grow the money over time) and use the other 50% to increase the total amount of money you invest with.

It's important to increase the amount of money you invest with over time. If you can build a substantial account, the opportunities you must take advantage of can be less risky and less time consuming. For example, an investor has an account containing $10,000 total; divided into two investments ($5,000 each); an 8% return on each position would give $400 profit per position. Now, let's say the investor has gradually built up their account to $30,000 over the years and once again divided their investment account into two positions ($15,000 per position). For the investor to make $400 profit per position like in the above example; only a 2.66% return would be needed ($400 / $15,000 = 2.66%). This is the advantage investors have when working with larger amounts of capital. It is much easier to make a 2.66% return on an investment than it is to make an 8% return.

I always tell investors that their goal is to build up the amount of money they invest with because it will ultimately allow them to make more money with less effort, quicker turn-around times, and substantially less risk. Think of a hedge fund manager picking a company and investing $1 million into a position. If they can make just 1% profit on that stock position, they will have a $10,000 profit; not a bad return for a stock moving only 1% higher. Most hedge funds deal with a lot more than $1 million on a position, so just imagine if the stock goes up 3-5%. For an investor with a $20,000 position in a stock, realizing a $10,000 profit would take a whopping 50% return. Now, you can see the difference in risk and effort; waiting for a stock to go up 50% as opposed to 1% for the same profit.

Earlier we discussed the power of having available cash in your investment account which enables you to capitalize on opportunities as they arise. Often investments can take a while to produce profits. By having available cash in your account, you won't have to exit an existing position prematurely (to free up some cash) if you see another investment opportunity develop in another stock.

I generally recommend having 15-25% of your investment account as cash. Implementing this rule would mean that your investment account should never have less than 15% of its total value as cash. The percentage of cash can increase, but never fall below 15%. Remember, we keep a significant percentage of our investment account as cash primarily for two reasons: to put ourselves in a position to seize opportunities as they arise and to also limit our risk and exposure by not putting all our money in the market.

Below is a formula on how to allocate our realized profits after a successful investment.

Formula for profit allocation (distribution):

$2,000 total profit made on an investment in Company ABC =

A) 50% of the total profit ($1,000):

Put this into a savings or checking account; possibly into a fixed income instrument like a CD (Certificate of Deposit) account. You have essentially taken out 50% of your profits and put them into an account(s) that is separate and unrelated to your investment account. You are locking in a percentage of your profits by not exposing them to the market entirely.

B) Remaining 50% of the total profit ($1,000):

This portion of the profit remains in the investment account. Concretely how an investor chooses to allocate this money within their investment account (whether to keep it as available cash or to reinvest it) is completely up to them. As you exit either winning or losing investment positions your total account value will vary over time. However, it is important to keep good structure in the account; no less than 15% of the account as cash. The cash percentage in your account will increase immediately after you sell a position; which is fine, but the goal is to never dip below the threshold of 15%. Some investors may choose to keep a higher percentage of their account as cash. This varies from investor to investor; however, I do not recommend that this value dips below 15% as a good risk management tactic. (end of part B)

If you recall earlier in the book we talked about taking advantage of variables we can control as investors, like our timing. As investors we have direct control over how we allocate our money between different investments and cash. Use variables you can control to your advantage.

Now, let's get back to risk management and how you should best divide up your investment portfolio. My general rule for any level of investor is to have no more than 10-15% of an investment account (based on total account value, including cash) dedicated to a single investment position. Remember it is smart risk management not to put all your eggs in one basket. Your investment account should be broken down into 10-15% per investment position and 15-25% as cash of the overall account value. So, let's use an account with a total capital worth of $100,000 as an example. We will assume you keep 25% (the upper range) of your $100,000 account as cash.

This means that $25,000 of your $100,000 investment account will be cash. The rest of the $75,000 in your investment account would be divided between various stock positions. So, let's say you are in seven different investment positions (of equal value upon initial investment) at a given point in time. The $75,000 would be broken down into approximately $10,714 per position ($75,000 / 7 positions = $10,714.28 per position). Having $10,714 per position would mean that each investment is 10.71% of the total account value ($10,714 / $100,000 = 0.107 or 10.7%).

The investment account discussed in the above paragraph is broken down in the correct manner. There is an appropriate percentage of the account dedicated to cash and each individual investment does not exceed the 10-15% limit upon initial investment. Obviously, as investors it is not necessary to have each investment equal to exactly 10% of the account value. However, it is not recommended for a single investment to exceed 15% of the total account value upon initial investment.

You must keep in mind that when we talk about a single investment accounting for 10% of the total account value we are referring to the total amount of capital (money) dedicated to the investment in the beginning of the investment cycle (when the shares are first purchased). For example, if the initial investment in Company ABC doubles in value after a period of time; the percentage of the total account value the position in Company ABC accounts for will increase drastically relative to the entire account (assuming the other positions stay relatively stable or go down in value).

If a stock goes up and it begins to account for a larger percentage of the total account value, as investors we should not downsize the winning position (of course we should lock in profits at some point as we discussed earlier) just to meet the general rule of having no more than 10-15% of the total account value allocated to one position. The principle behind the 10-15% per position applies when a stock is initially purchased relative to the total account value at the time of purchase.

Also, if an investment grows considerably the percentage of cash relative to the entire account could decrease substantially. Again, when we consider our 15-25% range for cash in our account, we are talking about when an investment(s) is initially made. If an investment in your portfolio grows significantly and reduces the percentage of cash to 8% of the total account; it doesn't mean, we must sell our winning position to increase our cash percentage. What this means is that unless you introduce more cash from an external source into your account, you should not be buying more stocks when your total account is only 8% cash. So, the cash can be increased by either external funding or the sale of investments in due time (which would both increase your cash percentage).

Earlier we talked about the best way to exit a winning position, which usually involves selling a stock in percentage portions of the total investment. This strategy is not implemented to downsize the position but rather to lock in profits on a percentage of the investment. Once again, the 10-15% rule applies to an investment when it is initially executed relative to the total account value at the time of investment. We always have to look at the ever-changing account value as various positions move up and down in value and adjust our future investments and cash balance to fall within our percentage parameters.

Limiting how much money you have invested in a single stock minimizes risk and exposure in case a particular stock underperforms. A well-diversified portfolio with strict percentage limitations per investment (along with a significant cash percentage) becomes very durable in the face of adverse market conditions and the underperformance of individual stocks. Basically, no one or two underperforming stocks (depending on how many total positions you have) should carry enough "weight" or influence to significantly affect a well-balanced portfolio that is built around the concepts of risk management, diversification, and capital preservation.

Chapter 30: Perception Part 1 (A Shift in Confidence)

Let's get back to identifying how best to capitalize on investment opportunities when they arise. The question I get asked the most is; how does one know when a stock is presenting a good investment opportunity? We can't just say for instance that a 10% drop in stock price must signal a great buying opportunity or a stock has been on the rise for several months, so it will probably continue in that direction. Rather we must perform some more analysis. Sometimes even large established companies have periods of prolong downtrends in stock price that don't necessarily signal good investment opportunities.

Legendary investor Robert Wilson in a 1985 interview once said, "The only way one makes money in the stock market is when the markets' perception of a stock changes." - Robert Wilson

Sometimes down trends in stock price in a company happen for various reasons like; underperformance of the company, change of investor perception, more competition for the company, the stock temporarily falling out of favor with investors, changing consumer trends, investor selling after dividends are paid out, profit taking by investors, a market correction/crash, limited company growth in the future, the stock reaching a P/E ratio that no longer presents a good value, and manipulation.

In contrast, stocks usually move upwards for the opposite side of the reasons listed above like: good company earnings/good performance, a stock that is selling at a bargain based on the P/E ratio, predicted future growth in the company, strong competitive advantage, low unemployment statistics that come out and raise general market sentiment etc.

However, all these catalysts translate into the bigger picture of either positive or negative investor perception; and investor perception is what ultimately moves stocks. If an investor can consistently identify the tipping point in any stock where perception will shift, that investor would have found the goose that lays the golden egg.

Sometimes a company's stock doesn't necessarily have to reach bargain prices for future investors to begin expressing interest in the stock. Or a company could be trading at a high valuation (high P/E ratio) but investors still view it as an investment opportunity predicting higher stock prices fueled by company growth in years to come. The market is made up of people governed by their psychologies. So, when investors think a stock could be a good investment opportunity the perception around the stock has shifted.

Besides evaluating fundamentals like P/E ratio, revenue, gross profit margins, net income etc.; it is also key to understand that investors can have a change of perception whether positive or negative without any clear numerical factor or catalyst. When the general perception changes, usually so does the stock price. A change in investor perception can happen for a wide variety of reasons.

The reason investor perception can change may be as simple as the price per share a company's stock is selling for. For example, an investor can see that Ford (F) stock is currently trading around $9 per share. The investor may say to themselves; "Well it's a big company and I don't see the stock price staying this low forever. It's pretty cheap so I could buy many shares and if it goes up I will make a decent profit." If enough people think like this concerning Ford (F) stock, the perception can shift toward the positive side. When investor perception shifts so do stock prices. Therefore it is important to not only perform fundamental analysis on a company but to also look at the big picture and consider how other investors may perceive a company and its stock. The change of investor perception is the change of investor confidence. When confidence rises investors tend to buy stocks and when confidence goes down investors generally sell.

Some down trends can last for a few hours, while others can last for several months and sometimes even years. The general rule I have for investing in blue-chip companies is; don't buy on significant down trends. A down trend is not to be confused with a sharp decline in price caused by a catalyst (like "bad" news or political tensions) or any event that causes general investor concern and panic in the markets. My general rule is to buy blue-chip stocks in overreaction situations especially when there is a slight upward recovery and general stabilization in share price after the initial reaction has taken place.

My general strategy is to invest in blue-chip stocks and/or any type of stock (whether the company is large, medium, or small by market capitalization) with strong fundamentals in two scenarios.

1) In over reaction situations where the sharp decrease in stock price is unwarranted.

And/or

2) When future growth is clear for the company in the long term (this mostly applies to small and medium sized companies with strong fundamentals and great promise for the future). Large companies also often have room for growth and should not be written off as companies that should be invested in only when overreaction situations occur. (end of scenario 2)

Most overreactions can be viewed as investment opportunities when the stock price begins to show resistance or bottoming out. This is when the down trend and stock price begin to level off and show stability with some small fluctuations but no clear up or down direction in share price. Meaning if a stock drops in share price by say 12% on a sharp decline, it should eventually begin to level off at the new price level possibly moving up and down a few percent but generally stabilizing in price.

This is referred to as resistance (basically the price doesn't seem to "want" to go any lower) when looking at stock charts and performing technical analysis. The resistance usually shows that the buyers and sellers of a stock are in a period of stagnation; meaning the supply and demand to buy and sell shares has basically leveled off after a significant drop. Usually during periods of resistance and price stabilization the perception among investors begins to change.

It is usually a good sign for an investor when a significant drop in price followed by a stabilization period begins to slowly exhibit movement toward the upside (share price begins to creep upward). This is usually seen as a sign of confidence buildup in investors who are beginning to have a change of perception and believing the stock is presenting an opportunity to recover in price.

As investors we must understand that obviously we are not the only ones looking for a good opportunity to buy shares at a bargain price. When you see any opportunity, understand that thousands of others also may see an opportunity to buy shares. The more people that identify the current price of a stock as a potential opportunity the higher the chance you will be able to capitalize on the opportunity and turn a profit. Remember, the stock market moves based on the principal of supply and demand. If enough investors believe a stock has reached a price where it is a good bargain (at least according to them) the demand for the stock will be high. Meaning there will be many interested buyers/investors in the stock placing their bids to buy shares. When the demand to buy a stock exceeds the demand to sell a stock, the stock price will move up.

After you spend a significant time in the stock market you will see just how quickly investor perception can change. This phenomenon applies to stocks when they move either up or down in price. For example, a stock maybe performing poorly and go down 15% during the course of three weeks. You will see comments on stock boards saying how bad the stock is and how it's practically worthless. If the same stock moves 3-4% higher after the initial decline you will see a huge shift in how investors perceive the stock, they once deemed as worthless. Suddenly, the stock becomes great and there is a lot of positive talk and posts about the company. Quite frankly, most investors do not value a stock based on fundamental analysis, but rather if the stock is moving upwards or is in decline.

The reason I mention this is because achieving success in the stock market is not an exact science but rather an art. You must sometimes get into the mentality of other investors and what they may see in a stock whether it is moving up, down, or stabilizing in price. Besides performing the essential fundamental analysis, you must ask yourself how other potential investors will view a stock at a given moment in time. Will they view the stock as an investment opportunity, a reason to sell, or just hold on to the stock?

Chapter 31: Perception Part 2 (Hammer and Nail)

Think about a nail that is being hammered into a piece of wood. The deeper the nail goes into the piece of wood the more difficult it becomes to remove it with the reverse part of the hammer (the claw). In contrast, as one pulls the nail further and further out of the wood the nail becomes easier to remove as it moves in increments closer and closer towards the surface of the wood.

Over the years I have come up with an analogy to explain how investor perception works regarding stocks by using the hammer and nail analogy. The basis of the analogy is the way stocks are impacted by either negative or positive news/events. When negative news or general market corrections occur, these events (catalysts) can drive a stock lower in price (or the nail deeper into the wood).

When negative catalysts occur repeatedly; the "nail" or stock is driven deeper and deeper into the wood making it more difficult to remove. On the other hand, positive results or news can have the opposite effect on a stock; the price of the stock rises (the nail is pulled further out of the wood). The more repeatedly positive catalysts influence a stock the further and further the nail is pulled out of the wood toward the surface. As the nail (stock) nears closer to the surface, a good piece of news can send it soaring higher because there is very little resistance/friction for the nail near the surface of the wood.

The deeper the nail goes the harder it will be to pull out and conversely the higher the nail sits near the surface of the wood the easier and quicker it will rise or come out of the wood. The driving of the nail into the wood represents a stock moving down in price and investor perception and confidence decreasing in increments in reaction to news and/or events in the stock market/company that negatively affect the stock. On the other hand, the nail getting removed in increments out of the wood represents the stock moving up in price and investor confidence/perception rising in increments as it is affected by positive news and/or events.

I have witnessed many stocks in companies small, medium, and large affected by the principles behind the "hammer and nail" analogy. You will often see a penny stock and the company behind it that has not yet proven itself (in terms of profitability) affected by this principle. A bad quarterly report, followed by global financial tensions, and a lack of updates from the company can drive the stock price lower and lower (or the nail deeper into the wood with each piece of negative news). When a piece of good news for the company finally does surface often times it does not have the expected effect of rising the stock significantly higher in price. The reason behind this is because investors have lost almost all confidence and trust in the company. One piece of news often times does not have enough "pull" to increase the stock price significantly against all the friction of low investor perception and trust.

I mention this as basically a warning to investors looking to start positions in unproven companies. By no means am I discouraging investors from taking positions in smaller companies that could have great returns with future growth. However, be cautious when investing in an unproven company and understand that stocks often move higher when the "friction" is low and investor confidence in the company is high and/or rising.

I have also seen small companies explode in stock price as a series of good news raises the "nail' further and further toward the top. One piece of good news in a company where investor confidence/perception is already high can send the stock price soaring (because there is very little friction left). This is not to say that a company that has been experiencing tough times cannot soar in stock price after one piece of significant good news. However, be cautious about the general situation you are investing your money in and keep in mind that other investors may have lost most of their confidence in the company and are reluctant to buy its shares.

Therefore, my investment philosophy is primarily based around investing in established blue-chip companies when an overreaction takes place. I like to invest in solid companies after the first piece of "bad" news affects the stock. Because perception and trust in the company is already high (the nail is not driven deep into the wood), the chance and ease with which the stock will rebound in a strong company is high. Again, when I refer to "bad" news; it is not something that is fundamental like decreasing revenues; but rather an event the causes unwarranted selling of the stock. I try to even avoid investing in strong companies if they have been repeatedly hammered by bad news because the recovery in share price after many blows to the stock is less likely. However, I always perform fundamental analysis and focus on the big picture when investing.

This is not to say that I only invest in blue-chip companies when they fall in price. I will often invest in a blue-chip company that has been steadily rising in stock price based on fundamental analysis and the prospect of continued growth. For example, a large company I see growth opportunity in that has been on the steady rise is Visa (V). I'm writing this section on 10/12/2018 and the current price of Visa (V) stock is approximately $138 per share. I see great opportunity in this stock, so I place a market order for 50 shares; my order is executed at a price of $138.159 per share on 10/12/2018. Visa (V) is a company with great fundamentals and has strong potential for future growth.

Investment Goal for Visa (V): Price target (PT) of $160-$180 per share.

Interesting fact: 80% of the entire world population still transacts on a cash basis. Along with rising revenues and a rock-solid business model; this tells me that there is plenty of room for growth in the company as it expands into undeveloped markets.

A series of over-reactions and bad news can even drive a strong company's stock lower. If the lowered price in the stock still presents a strong investment based on fundamentals like P/E and increasing sales I will most likely invest. Remember, "bad" news can be specific to a company or there could be general negative news/events that affects the market as a whole. Negative news that affects the markets as a whole usually can lead to great investment opportunities because this type of news usually does not reflect directly on the company in question.

Think about the fact that every year the market can experience multiple significant corrections for various reasons. Strong blue-chip stocks that have had a steady rise in price or are perhaps stagnant in their stock price can be corrected to bargain prices as the market dips as a whole. This phenomenon is almost guaranteed to happen because the market experiences corrections at least once during a single year. Also, various sectors (home improvement, automotive, technology etc.) can experience their own corrections multiple times during a single year, all these events can lead to investment opportunities.

Chapter 32: General Investment Rules

These six rules will save you a lot of time, money, and frustration as an investor.

1. As an investor you should never chase a stock. This happens every day in the stock market and investors end up losing big. Let's say you are looking at a stock and it's moving up substantially and rather quickly. It's up 10% in the morning and continues to run-up another 5% after lunch time. A lot of investors conclude that the stock is on "fire" and they can't miss out on the run (FOMO – fear of missing out). This is probably one of the best ways to lose money as an investor. Never chase a stock because it's almost impossible to predict where the top will be. I have explained this rule to investors many times over the years, but when these situations arise they tend to ignore it out of greed and irrational emotion. Ingrain this rule in your mind and always stick to it, no matter how tempting a stock looks as is soars to the top.

Remember there are investors big and small in the stock market all looking to make a profit. What if two minutes after you bought the stock a hedge fund decides to unload a $1 million position to lock in their profits? Well the stock is going to drop significantly, and you will be stuck in a bad position. So, the golden rule is never to chase a stock because you think that you may miss out on the run. Once you see a stock start moving drastically upwards it is basically too late. If investing was as easy as buying a stock that is moving rapidly upwards, everyone would be a multi-millionaire.

2. The next general rule is never trying to catch a falling stock (never try to catch a "falling knife"); this rule will always save you a lot of money. Sometimes an investor sees a falling stock and tries to buy it on the way down looking for a bargain price. It's almost impossible to identify where the bottom will be. Again, we only buy on opportunities that have leveled off or began to show resistance. Meaning the price has reached a low point but has now begun to stabilize. The duration of the stabilization period may vary in time from a few hours to several months. What you are ultimately looking for is, for the price to stabilize and possibly begin to show signs of an uptrend. The stock does not always have to start rising in price (uptrend) for you to make an investment. You must look at the big picture when a stock falls in price. Is it presenting a good investment opportunity based on the fundamentals we have covered in this book?

3. Always perform fundamental and technical analysis on a company. Without looking at the core fundamentals of a company it is virtually impossible to truly understand what is happening within the company and how the stock price may be affected by key fundamental data. When performing technical analysis always keep in mind how other investors might view the current price of a stock and whether they will equate the current price as an opportunity to invest, sell, or hold. Do your research, invest - don't speculate.

4. Learn to cut your losses. A lot of investors cannot get themselves to sell a losing position. Even the best investors occasionally make mistakes. If after a significant amount of time an investment is not producing, you should strongly consider selling it or at least a portion of the original investment. Often investors hold onto losing stocks for far too long because they cannot admit to themselves that they have made a mistake. If a company is truly underperforming and its future prospects look grim, be intelligent enough to understand that it's possible to make a mistake and be honest with yourself – cut your losses. Or perhaps you misvalued a stock and bought it at a high price that is unlikely to ever turn a profit. Don't let your pride stop you from selling a losing position that adversely affects your entire investment portfolio.

5. Don't sell in and out of stocks too frequently. A lot of investors lose money because they are too easily distracted by everything that's going on in the stock market. They will buy several stocks and if those stocks do not produce quick profits they begin to look elsewhere. Often investors succumb to boredom and exit their positions prematurely and for a loss; to then jump into another stock they deem as worthy. When the "new and good" stock doesn't perform the way they initially expected they sell that position and the cycle continues. Investors like this rack up significant losses over time and ultimately move backwards. My advice is, do your research on a company and be patient enough to wait for the reward.

6. Do not allocate too much money/capital to a single investment. Often investors have a false conviction that one particular stock in their portfolio will surely make them a lot of money. Often times their conviction is incorrect and when that one stock underperforms their entire portfolio could be down 50%. Allocate (distribute) your money wisely per investment and never place a huge importance on a single stock to perform. Limit your position size to 10-15% of your investment portfolio per investment.

Chapter 33: Dividend Reinvestment and Compound Interest

This will be the last chapter of the book, but it is of great importance and should not be overlooked. In Chapter 29: Building an Investment Portfolio (Part 2), we talked about putting 50% of the profits you make from any investment into a non-investment related account, while the other 50% of the profits should remain in the investment account. I strongly advise that part of the 50% that remains in the investment account should be partially dedicated to investments in stocks that pay steady and good dividends.

A cash dividend is a payment made by a company out of its earnings to investors in the form of cash; whether it be in the form of a check or electronic transfer. There are many strong and established companies that pay their shareholders good dividends for simply buying and holding their shares. Most American companies pay dividends on a quarterly basis. You will find that dividend payments are usually made by well-established and profitable companies. An established company with solid and stable earnings does not have to constantly reinvest in itself (or at least not as much as an up and coming company the needs to grow) and can often choose to share some of its profits with investors that are holding its stock.

Personally, I reinvest 10-15% of my profits (out of the 50% that remains in the investment account after a profit is made) into companies that pay dividends ranging from approximately 3-5% on an annual basis. Some of these companies have consistently increased their dividend payments for 40, 50, and even 60 years consecutively. I strongly recommend that as an investor you dedicate a percentage of your profits and reinvest them into dividend paying stocks. This strategy plays into building a strong portfolio that is centered around risk management, durability, diversification, and capital preservation.

The beauty about earning dividend payments is that you can reinvest the dividends once they are paid out; either back into the same company or into any other stock of your choice. If you choose to reinvest the dividends back into the same company that paid them out, you will be taking advantage of the powerful concept of compound interest. Collecting dividends on a profit (made from a previous investment or a dividend payment) by investing in a dividend paying company's' stock is basically making profits on top of profits.

The power of compound interest is clearly known and widely talked about in the investment world. Every time you reinvest your dividend payment back into the dividend paying company you will be collecting your next dividend payment based on a higher amount of capital/shares (the compound interest principal). Repeating the process of dividend reinvesting is extremely lucrative because every time you reinvest the dividend payment, you will be paid more money the next time the dividend payment date comes around based on a higher share count and an ever-increasing principal in the dividend paying stock.

Investing in companies that pay dividends should be done with the same principles we mentioned earlier in this book. Obviously even an investment in a dividend paying company can either move up and down in value as the stock price fluctuates. However, if you invest correctly you can benefit both from the growth of the stock itself and by collecting a dividend payment every quarter just by holding the stock.

Think of dividend payments as a salary that you earn. Once you invest in a dividend paying company you will have a salary that comes in every quarter as the dividend payment(s) is made. The more you invest and reinvest into dividend paying stocks the higher your salary will be. Many retirees who have a significant amount of money can live off dividend payments. Dividend payments will give your investment portfolio greater stability and increase your investment portfolios' returns (and make the returns almost guaranteed as far as the payments that come from dividend paying stocks). This strengthens our portfolio and makes it much more durable.

Final Thoughts

The field of investing has been covered in countless books over many decades. All investors have a slightly different approach to the world of finance and investing. Some investors put emphasis on short term gains while others focus on long-term growth. However, I believe that there is a common theme among all successful investors - past, present, and future. Investors who focus on the fundamental analysis of a company and use good risk management tactics are those who experience the greatest success. Remember, your first goal should always be to preserve the capital you initially invested, followed by making consistent returns and building your portfolio size over time. Thank you for purchasing this book and I hope that you gained some helpful knowledge and it was entertaining along the way!

Copyright © 2018 by Damir Dadachov.

All Rights Reserved.

References List

"Market manipulation." *Wikipedia*. Wikimedia Foundation Inc, 22 May 2018. Web. 15 Sept 2018. https://en.wikipedia.org/wiki/Market_manipulation

"Blue Chip." *Investopedia*. Investopedia, LLC., Web. 18 Sept 2018. https://www.investopedia.com/terms/b/bluechip.asp

"Walmart." *Wikipedia*. Wikimedia Foundation Inc, 29 Oct 2018. Web. 02 Sept 2018. https://en.wikipedia.org/wiki/Walmart

Russell, Jon. "Walmart completes its $16 billion acquisition of Flipkart." *TechCrunch*. Oath Tech Network, August 2018. Web. 19 Sept 2018. https://techcrunch.com/2018/08/20/walmart-flipkart-deal-done/

"Revenue." *Wikipedia*. Wikimedia Foundation Inc, 26 Sept 2018. Web. 13 Sept 2018. https://en.wikipedia.org/wiki/Revenue

Ross, Sean. "What items on the balance sheet are most important in fundamental analysis?." *Investopedia*. Investopedia, LLC., Web. 18 Sept 2018. https://www.investopedia.com/ask/answers/050615/what-items-balance-sheet-are-most-important-fundamental-analysis.asp

Phillips, Jack. "How does eBay make money?." *Quora*. Quora, 21 Feb 2017. Web. 15 Aug 2018. https://www.quora.com/How-does-eBay-make-money

"eBay Revenue, Profits – EBAY Annual Income Statement." *amigobulls.com*. Amigobulls, 15 August 2018. Web. 15 Aug 2018. https://amigobulls.com/stocks/EBAY/income-statement/annual

"eBay Revenue, Profits – EBAY Quarterly Income Statement." *amigobulls.com*. Amigobulls, 15 August 2018. Web. 15 Aug 2018. https://amigobulls.com/stocks/EBAY/income-statement/quarterly

eBay Balance Sheet – Quarterly (NASDAQ: EBAY)." *amigobulls.com*. Amigobulls, 15 August 2018. Web. 15 Aug 2018. https://amigobulls.com/stocks/EBAY/balance-sheet/quarterly

"Company Overview of HUYA Inc." *Bloomberg*. Bloomberg L.P., 24 Sept 2018. Web. 19 Sept 2018. https://www.bloomberg.com/research/stocks/private/snapshot.asp?privcapId=431096194

"HUYA Inc. ADR." *MarketWatch*. MarketWatch Inc, 19 Sept 2018. Web. 19 Sept 2018. https://www.marketwatch.com/investing/stock/huya/financials

"HUYA Inc. ADR." *MarketWatch*. MarketWatch Inc, 19 Sept 2018. Web. 19 Sept 2018. https://www.marketwatch.com/investing/stock/huya/financials/income/quarter

"HUYA Inc. ADR." *MarketWatch*. MarketWatch Inc, 19 Sept 2018. Web. 19 Sept 2018. https://www.marketwatch.com/investing/stock/huya/financials/balance-sheet/quarter

www.ingramcontent.com/pod-product-compliance
Lightning Source LLC
Chambersburg PA
CBHW020442220526
45464CB00002B/823